OUTSIDERS in a HEARING WORLD

A SOCIOLOGY OF DEAFNESS

PAUL C. HIGGINS

Foreword by Robert A. Scott

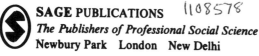

SAGE PUBLICATIONS
The Publishers of Professional Social Science
Newbury Park   London   New Delhi

For information address:

 SAGE Publications, Inc.
2455 Teller Road
Newbury Park, California 91320

SAGE Publications Ltd.
6 Bonhill Street
London EC2A 4PU
United Kingdom

SAGE Publications India Pvt. Ltd.
M-32 Market
Greater Kailash I
New Delhi 110 048 India

Printed in the United States of America

Library of Congress Cataloging in Publication Data

Higgins, Paul C.
    Outsiders in a hearing world

    (Sociological observations ; 10)
    Bibliography: p.
    1. Deaf. 2. Deafness–Social aspects.
I. Title. II. Series.
HV2395.H53   305   80-12150
ISBN 0-8039-1421-0
ISBN 0-8039-1422-9 (pbk.)

        94   15   14

Materials from Chapter 2, "The Deaf Community," have appeared in *Urban Life* Volume 8, Number 1 (April 1979) and are used here with the permission of Sage Publications. Materials from Chapter 4, "Deviance Among the Deaf," have appeared in *Pacific Sociological Review*, Volume 22, Number 1 (January 1979) and are used here with the permission of the Pacific Sociological Association and Sage Publications. Materials from Chapter 6, "Encounters with the Hearing," have appeared in *Symbolic Interaction* Volume 3, Number 1 (Spring 1980) and are used here with the permission of the Society for the Study of Symbolic Interaction.

Contents

To My Mother and Father
with Love

Foreword

Studies of people who are physically disabled have occupied an important place in the field of sociology of deviant behavior. Some of the most seminal insights into stigma have come out of research on the disabled. Our understanding of how and why communications between deviants and normals break down has been greatly advanced through studies of everyday interactions between the disabled and the nondisabled. We have learned much about the elusive fiber that keeps everyday, common, taken-for-granted reality intact through studying the handicapped, because of the special way in which their problems expose this fiber for our observation and analysis. Significant modifications in deviancy theory have been occasioned by the realization that the physically impaired, by virtue of their disability alone, are often treated as deviants in our society.

Much of this work has been done on just a few groups, notably amputees, persons with facial disfigurements, the crippled, the blind, and the deformed. Conspicuously missing until now are studies of the deaf. The sociological literature on deafness is meager in comparison to other disabled groups, and much of it is of limited value because it is anecdotal and speculative. Happily, this is no longer the case, for in this book Paul Higgins provides us with an informative introduction to the sociology of deafness. The true value of his study only becomes

apparent after we stop to consider why, for so long, the deaf have
escaped the attention of sociologists of deviant behavior.
The reason is not that deafness is rare in our society. Higgins reports
that there are about two million people in the United States who can
neither hear nor speak and another eleven million who have some type
of serious or severe hearing impairment. When we realize that the blind,
on whom sociologists have lavished considerably more attention, number no more than a million, of whom less than 50,000 are completely
unable to see, we begin to appreciate how neglectful our social science
community has been toward the deaf. The explanation for this has
much to do with understanding the place of the deaf in our society, and
this is precisely what Higgins's book is about. The plight of the deaf in
everyday life has implications for our ability to study them. Higgins
explains that in order to do research on this group, the researcher needs
to have special skills, and even then special problems arise. The sociologist who wishes to interview deaf persons must know how to communicate in sign language, a talent which requires considerable training.
In addition to mastering signing, the researcher must also be prepared
to abandon time-tested, familiar techniques of interviewing and data
collection. For example, it is very difficult for anyone to read sign
language while at the same time taking notes on what is being said, and,
of course, it is impossible to reply in sign language and continue to
write down what is being communicated. The usual substitutes for
note-taking, such as tape-recording, are of course useless in a conversation that is being signed, and also of very limited value with deaf
persons who speak and express themselves in tones that are not clear.
In place of these things one must rely on memory, trying to recall after
an interview is finished what was said by whom. Moreover, few deaf
people are able to use the telephone, and this means that it is difficult
to contact them directly. Once interview times are arranged there is no
easy way to change them in response to the inevitable contingencies of
life that disrupt daily schedules. As if this were not enough, among
many deaf people there is a wariness of the hearing and an understandable reluctance to open up to them. Many deaf people prefer to keep to
themselves and they are deeply suspicious of any hearing person who
displays an interest in them and their situation. And so, the deaf are
socially isolated from the hearing world and pose special communication difficulties for the sociologist who wishes to study them.
    Paul Higgins brings to this study a whole host of skills that have
enabled him to surmount many of these problems in a way that no
other social scientist before him has managed to do. Both his parents

are deaf and because of this he acquired an intimate familiarity with the problem of deafness from his earliest years. During his youth, his parents were actively involved in many of the activities of the deaf community and their involvement became an important part of his own life during the years he was growing up. Before going to Northwestern University to study sociology, he worked for a time as a counselor in a school for the deaf, and his enduring ties to the deaf community continue to be reinforced not only by his research but also by the fact that his wife is currently actively involved in work for the deaf. He is fluent in sign language and understands well the special problems of communication that can arise with deaf persons who can lipread and -speak. Through his parents he has been able to gain entree into the deaf community and in it enjoy the kind of legitimacy that few other hearing people have. Thus, he comes to this study well prepared to meet the technical difficulties it presents.

He is also well prepared in sociology, and he brings to his research a good grasp of basic sociological ideas. Conceptually, his study is set squarely in the midst of modern-day deviancy theory. Howard Becker's classic statement about outsiders provides the framework within which his analysis is conducted. This framework leads him to examine the special problems of identity, interaction, and social status confronting those who cannot hear as they live out their lives in a world which is heavily dependent on sound. His analysis is both rich and revealing. We learn, for example, that even though the problems of deafness may be invisible to many of us who hear, there is nevertheless a highly viable deaf community in America which provides an important rallying point of identity for many people. This community is large, very active, and extremely cohesive. For its members it supplies a context in which they preserve a keen sense of separateness from the hearing community. We learn that this community is divided into strata and cliques based upon common lines of social differentiation in our culture, such as age, sex, education, and ethnicity, as well as along lines of differentiation unique to the world of the deaf, such as those based upon preferred modes of communication, like signing, speaking, and lipreading. The community is both local and national in scope and for many of its members it is the central focus of their lives. In fact, it is so strong a force that some members of it, people who have belonged to deaf organizations for many years, who have regained their hearing through surgery or in other ways, conceal the fact that they are no longer deaf in order to continue to enjoy the companionship and sense of identity which the community provides them.

In this book we also learn about some of the problems of identity that confront the deaf. Higgins explains how people who lose their hearing come to identify with the deaf community and how that identity is managed. We are provided with insights into some of the problems the deaf encounter in their daily interactions with hearing people, why these interactions often go awry, and why deaf people therefore shy away from regular encounters with persons who are not like them. There is an interesting chapter on peddling among the deaf, how it is done, and how it is viewed by the different groups comprising the deaf community. We learn about the ways in which the stigma of deafness has its impact on people and how the deaf view their disability in contrast to the ways in which hearing people see it. In a chapter on the deaf in the hearing world we learn about some of the strategies deaf people use to conceal their problem, and overt situations in which it could become salient. And finally, in the appendix, Higgins discusses the multitude of problems involved in doing research on deaf people and how he tried to overcome them.

All in all, this book provides a long-overdue introduction to the social world of the deaf, an introduction framed in terms that allow the reader to relate the discussion to some of the central issues in the sociology of deviant behavior. For this reason, it is a welcome contribution to the field. And, as with any worthwhile study, it raises a variety of interesting questions for further research and writing: It invites us to learn more about how social life is experienced by those who must cope in a hearing environment in which they cannot fully participate; it prompts us to speculate about how the circumstance of the deaf is comparable to that of other disabled groups and how it is special; and it raises a host of questions, too numerous to mention here, about the impact of this disability on people who acquired it at different stages of their lives. These and other questions make it a book that will be of interest to a wide audience of persons in the social science community, and it is a pleasure for me to be able to provide this introductory foreword to it.

—Robert A. Scott
Princeton University

Acknowledgments

Research is rarely a solitary enterprise, even if the final product bears only one author's name. Assistance usually comes from many people. This book is based on a dissertation which I wrote while at Northwestern University. I thank Gary Albrecht, Howard S. Becker, and Andrew Gordon for their thoughtful comments and encouragement. As editor of the series in which this book appears, John M. Johnson has provided insightful suggestions for improving this work.

Without the help and the cooperation of the members of the deaf community and of the other respondents who shared their lives and experiences with me, this book would not have been possible. I deeply appreciate that cooperation.

My wife, Leigh, made the difficult periods of my research and writing seem not so difficult at all and made the exciting parts wonderful.

–P.C.H.

Introduction

Sociologists have conflicting views about using their own personal experiences as part of the research enterprise. Those experiences may have been cultivated as a sociologist or carried with the individual to sociology. Some sociologists argue that personal experiences and beliefs get in the way of objectivity. Therefore, such experiences must be minimized by relying on survey research techniques or experimental designs. Others recognize the importance of researchers' having first-hand experience with the people or situation that they are trying to understand, but warn the researchers not to become too involved lest they "go native," i.e., become so much a part of the scene which they are investigating that they can no longer reflect on what is happening. A few argue that personal experiences are and should be an important part of the sociologist's research (Gouldner, 1970; Douglas, 1976). Twenty years ago C. Wright Mills (1959: 196) argued that sociologists must use their life experiences in their intellectual work. Continually examining and interpreting those experiences become important parts of the sociologist's craft. Or as Jeffrey Riemer (1977: 467) noted:

Social science researchers too frequently neglect "at hand" knowledge and expertise they alone possess in the engineering of their research ventures. They often ignore or treat as ancillary their own unique biographies, life experiences, and situational familiarity when these could opportunistically serve as important sources for research ideas and data.

Certainly my own life experiences have greatly influenced this work. My parents are deaf. My wife teaches deaf children. I taught at a state school for the deaf for one year before I began graduate work in sociology. I mention these parts of my life because they have had a profound impact on my research and the book which I have written.

Sociologists do research on a wide variety of topics, as any undergraduate major knows. How do they select which topics to pursue? A cynic might answer that topics are chosen because they are likely to be funded. Those which are not funded do not get investigated. Some sociologists develop research projects in order to help fill what they perceive to be a gap in sociological knowledge. They are developing the discipline. Others simply try to make sense out of their own experiences or the experiences of those whom they are familiar with. In doing so, they may place those experiences within a broader social context. They transform personal experiences into sociological issues.

The following chapters are the results of my research of the Chicago area deaf community. Those chapters are an examination of the lives of deaf people in a world which is not deaf.

As I reflect upon my own research, I realize that I was not only trying to understand deaf people and their world. Certainly I was trying to do that. I was also trying, though, to understand my parents. I do not mean that in a personal sense. Rather, I was trying to locate their lives and experiences, as I knew them, within a larger historical and social context. To do that, I had to go beyond their own lives to the diverse experiences of those who are outsiders in a hearing world.

Most situations of interest to sociologists are complex. They involve the many perspectives of the various people in the situation, perspectives which often conflict. Ideally, sociologists should try to understand all of those viewpoints in doing their research. Thus, in a detailed study of prostitution, a sociologist could examine the experiences, activities, and perspectives of prostitutes, pimps, patrons, police, politicians and the public. Each is involved in the scene in a different way. Even among each group there are widely varying experiences. Sociologists, though, are constrained by time, funds, the availability of help, personal interests, and so on. Thus situations are typically researched from one or two (certainly a limited number of) viewpoints, though they need not be (Douglas, 1976). However, situations must be investigated from someone's viewpoint. As Howard Becker (1967: 245) observed:

> We must always look at the matter from someone's point of view. The scientist who proposes to understand society must, as Mead long ago pointed out, get into the situation enough to have a perspective on it. And it is likely that his perspective will be greatly affected by whatever positions are taken by any or all of the other participants in that varied situation.

In order fully to understand the lives of deaf people, we must examine their experiences as well as the hearing world within which they live. Diverse experiences, activities, and perspectives characterize both groups. Neither group is homogeneous. Nor is it always easy to know who belongs to which group. Most of us, though, are much more familiar with the perspectives of the hearing public, because we are among its members, than we are with the experiences of the deaf. And much previous writing and thinking about the deaf has been from the perspective of the hearing. Therefore, it makes sense to examine the world as deaf people experience it.

Further, as will become clear in the following chapters, the assumptions and practices of those who hear have had a profound impact on the lives of those who do not hear. Rarely, though, have members of the hearing world carefully examined their assumptions about or practices toward the deaf. Of course, assumptions are ideas which people take for granted. That is how the world is supposed to be. Those assumptions have not only limited the lives of the deaf. As long as they remain unexamined, the hearing are also constrained by them. Alternative perspectives and practices are never considered. To recognize those assumptions and to understand them fully requires a critical examination. Yet is difficult to be critical of ideas which have been taken for granted for so long. Often we are not even aware that we are relying on them. The deaf, though, continually confront those assumptions. Therefore, in examining the social world of the deaf, we not only better understand their lives, but we also better understand the world created by the hearing.

As Joseph Gusfield (1976: 32) makes clear:

> It is this capacity to recognize the context of unexamined assumptions and accepted concepts that is among the most valuable contributions through which social science enables human beings to transcend the conventional and create new approaches and policies.

In the following chapters I have tried to understand the world as deaf people do. Throughout, I explain their lives as they live them. I use their words (and signs) and actions to depict their world. Taking their perspective, however, does not mean that there are not other perspectives as well, most notably the perspective of hearing people. Even among the deaf there are diverse views. Nor does it mean that hearing people cannot help us understand what it means to be deaf. The experiences of hearing people who are familiar with the deaf can complement and question, but should not be substituted for, the experiences of deaf people. In order to understand the deaf, we must consider their viewpoint. While we may or may not accept it, we certainly must be empathic with it (Matza, 1969: 18).

Chapter 1 establishes the framework for the book. In a world where sounds are vitally important, deaf people are outsiders. They are also outsiders in a more profound sense. That world of sounds has been created and is dominated by those who hear. Thus, the deaf are outsiders in a world which is largely controlled by the hearing. However, other people also contend with a world which is largely controlled by someone else. Black Americans are outsiders in a white world. Gays are outsiders in a straight world. The blind are outsiders in a sighted world, and so on. Through examining the experiences of deaf people, we may better understand outsiders in general, and by examining the lives of other outsiders, we may better understand those who are outsiders in a hearing world.

Chapter 2 is an examination of the deaf community. A hearing impairment is a necessary, though not a sufficient, condition for membership within a deaf community. The great majority of hearing-impaired people do not become members of deaf communities. This chapter and the remaining chapters are about the lives of those who are members.

Chapter 3 analyzes the identity of those who are members of the deaf community. Because hearing is so important within the larger world, the inability to hear is the salient feature of members' identities. Members cannot easily forget the overwhelming emphasis of their parents and teachers to learn to speak and to lipread (i.e., to become like the hearing). Nor can they overlook the very real drawbacks of being deaf in a hearing world. At the same time, though, members of the deaf community identify with the deaf. They feel a sense of belonging among fellow members which is not found within the hearing world. Therefore, they are likely to be ambivalent about their deafness.

Chapter 4 investigates the deviance of peddling within the deaf community. The selling of small items such as pens, key chains, or sign language cards by deaf people is offensive to most members of the deaf community. The reasons for the deviance of peddling help us understand how the deaf community views itself within a hearing world.

Chapter 5 explores the stigmatization of the deaf. In a world which takes physical ability for granted, those who are disabled are discredited. Stigmatization often leads to unsatisfying interaction for the deaf in a hearing world. The deaf community is partly a response to the stigma of being deaf.

Chapter 6 examines encounters between the deaf and the hearing. Interaction between the deaf and the hearing is often strained and awkward due to the impact of deafness and its accompanying limitations on social interaction. The effects of deafness, however, are only fully realized within the assumptions and routine practices of hearing people. The assumptions and routine practices usually successfully maintain interaction, but they often lead to confusion when applied to the deaf.

In the Conclusion, I make explicit two types of interdependencies which have been implied throughout the book. First, the deaf community, the identity of its members, and the interaction between the deaf and the hearing are interrelated. Each influences the other. Second, being deaf and being able to hear are interrelated The *deaf* community and the identity of *deaf* people arise out of the deaf's experiences in a hearing world. Although hearing is usually taken for granted, the full significance of being able to hear is in contrast to those who cannot hear. The historical relationship between the deaf and the hearing is changing. Therefore, there is reason to be cautiously optimistic about the future of outsiders in a hearing world.

In the Research Appendix I describe how I gathered data about the experiences of members of the Chicago area deaf community. Throughout the book, incidents involving and quotations of various deaf and hearing people appear. Some of the quotations are not grammatically correct English—that is, after all, how people communicate. More importantly, I have tried to maintain the anonymity of those who shared their lives with me. I am not particularly concerned that sociologists or the hearing world would recognize these people. Rather, other deaf people may recognize them, which could be embarrassing. Therefore, all the personal names which appear are fictitious. Information which would have identified specific people was generally deleted. In a few instances, the deletion of such information would have made the data useless. Thus, I suspect that a few deaf people can be recognized by fellow outsiders in a hearing world. I trust that I did no harm to them.

1

OUTSIDERS IN
A HEARING WORLD

Most of us live in a world of sounds. We are surrounded by all kinds of sounds. Often we take them for granted. We give them little thought until we unexpectedly do not hear them. Nevertheless, we thoroughly depend on sounds to get through our everyday lives. We would be lost without them.

Our day begins with sound, is regulated by sounds, and is interrupted by sounds. We awaken to alarm clocks, change classes according to bells, and are distracted by ringing telephones. Sirens and alarms warn us of potential danger. Yet, so does an odd-sounding automobile engine or heartbeat. Sounds please us as well as irritate us. Young children's laughter, the crashing of waves on a beach, and our favorite songs give us joy. Barking dogs, thundering airplanes, and noisy neighbors annoy us. Sounds fill up our day.

Some complain that there are too many sounds, that there is too much noise. In defense they have coined the phrase, "noise pollution," and passed local ordinances to reduce the level of some of the sounds around them. They may even warn us how much noise different products create by testing and labeling the products. However, most of us would agree that our lives would be very different without sounds. Many of us could not even imagine what it would be like.

Most importantly, we communicate through sounds—by means of telephones, radios, intercom systems, and loud-speakers. Even television, which seems to be a very visual medium, often makes little sense without sound. Try watching a television program with the sound turned off. And, of course, we talk. Thus, much of our everyday lives is based on the assumption that we can hear. Yet, what becomes of those who cannot hear, those who are deaf? They live within a world of sounds but are not fully part of that world. In this very obvious sense, they are outsiders in a hearing world.

The deaf are outsiders in a related but more profound sense as well. They are not only outsiders because they miss out on a world of sounds, because they cannot hear. They are also outsiders in a world largely created and controlled by those who do hear. The deaf live within a world which is not of their own making, but one which they must continually confront. This second notion of the deaf as outsiders deserves much greater discussion.

Among sociologists, Howard Becker (1963) popularized the concept "outsider." After noting that all groups make rules which define some behavior as right and other behavior as wrong, Becker (1963: 1) observed:

> When a rule is enforced, the person who is supposed to have broken it may be seen as a special kind of person, one who cannot be trusted to live by the rules agreed on by the group. He is regarded as an *outsider*.

Groups do, indeed, create rules. In a broader sense, however, they create their reality. Rules which define what is right and wrong are an important part, but only a part, of that reality. Thus, I want to broaden Becker's notion of outsiders in order that it can become a useful framework for understanding the deaf.

People create reality. I do not mean that just in some abstract sense, although what people do is often significantly based on abstract ideas of what is good and bad, what is normal and abnormal, what people are like and should be like, and so on. With regard to the deaf, these abstract ideas have been very important, as we will see momentarily. Rather, through specific activities of everyday life, people create the world within which they and others live. It is with these specific activities that outsiders must contend. People build and destroy. They hire and fire. They establish schools and decide what will be taught in them, how it will be taught, and who will be taught. For all kinds of positions they set up criteria and requirements and then evaluate whether others meet them or not. They praise and they condemn. They legislate against certain activities, but allow and even encourage others. They wage war, but profess to seek peace. They write books, but ban others. And so it goes. Creating reality is a complex and ever changing process which we may never fully understand. It has been and continues to be a process controlled largely by those who hear.

HISTORICAL FOUNDATIONS

The hearing world has existed for thousands of years. Through all those years, the deaf have largely been outsiders. As I noted before, in creating reality, people base their actions on abstract ideas. With regard to the deaf, the hearing have based their actions on ideas and assumptions about what it means not to be able to hear, and consequently what those who cannot hear must be like. Although it may be perilous to condense history into a few pages, let me briefly highlight the historical relationship between the hearing and the deaf.[1]

Put simply, hearing people have assumed that the deaf are not fully competent human beings. This assumption has concerned primarily those born deaf or who became deaf at an early age, and particularly those who could not speak. This assumption has taken various forms, some more and some less extreme. Yet, in all cases, it has had a profound impact on the world created by the hearing, a world with which the deaf must contend.

In its earliest and most extreme form, the assumption was based on the following argument: Thinking cannot develop

without language. Language, in turn, cannot develop without
speech. (Language and speech were often seen as synon-
ymous.) Speech cannot develop without hearing. Therefore,
those who cannot hear cannot think. The early Greeks and
Romans applied this argument primarily to those born deaf,
because they noticed that those who became deaf later in life
did not lose their speech, language, or thinking abilities.
Aristotle concluded that those born deaf were also dumb.
They were dumb in the sense that they could vocalize, but
could not speak. Whether he thought that the deaf were
senseless as well is not clear, but early translators often
interchanged the Greek words for "speechless" and "senseless." Thus, Pliny the Elder wrote in his *Natural History*,
"There are no persons born deaf that are not also dumb."

Many researchers and professionals in the fields of deafness, audiology and psychology now recognize that each
premise of the argument as well as the conclusion is false.[2]
Intimate, everyday experiences with the deaf also show the
absurdity of the conclusion. However, ideas which have been
around for thousands of years are often difficult to abandon
completely. Consequently, the authors of a widely used text-
book in social psychology argue that until the child

> begins to comprehend and use conventional speech, his human-
> ness is only partial. The child becomes socialized when he has
> acquired the ability to communicate with others and to influence
> and be influenced by them through the use of speech [Linde-
> smith et al., 1975: 239].

These ideas about the relationship between hearing and
thinking and about the competence of the deaf strongly
influenced the world which the hearing created. In very
specific ways, these ideas influenced how the hearing acted
toward the deaf in everyday life. For example, early Hebrew
law warned:

> If one exposes his cattle to the sun, or he places them in the
> custody of a deaf-mute, a fool, or a minor, and they break away
> and do damage, he is liable [see Bender, 1970: 19].

Those who were deaf and could not speak were not allowed to own real estate, could not act as a witness (all testimony was oral), could not be validly married, but also could not be punished if they or their animals injured someone. Those who could hear but could not speak were under no such restrictions.

The Romans deprived those deaf who could not speak of all legal rights. They were not allowed to make wills, could not grant freedom from slavery, and required a guardian over all their affairs. The Christian Church from St. Augustine's time into the Middle Ages believed that the deaf could not achieve immortality because they could not speak the sacraments.

Early laws of the 1800s in America reflected similar views about the deaf. In New York, those who were deaf from birth and could not speak were not allowed to vote. Many states held that the deaf were incompetent to make a contract, but also were not criminally responsible for their behavior. The deaf were also viewed as a potential burden upon the community. In the early 1800s, owners of all ships arriving in the United States were required to report to port authorities whether deaf and other dependent persons were on board, and pay sufficient bond to keep them from becoming public charges. Alabama and Georgia enacted similar laws to prevent carnivals from bringing deaf people with them and then abandoning them in a local town (Best, 1943). Whether denied legal rights, paternalistically cared for so as not to be taken advantage of, or guarded against lest they become a burden, the deaf were treated as incompetent. Of course, such treatment no doubt led some deaf people to become incompetent. A self-fulfilling prophecy was at work.

Gradually, but by no means completely, the assumption that the deaf could not think gave way to less extreme views of their incompetence. No doubt that assumption gave way as small, tentative programs were developed to educate the deaf. In the United States those programs slowly developed during the 1800s, though they had begun at least two hundred years earlier in Europe. The history of the education of the deaf in the United States and elsewhere is both complex and important for understanding the lives of deaf people. In some of the following chapters, I will analyze the impact of educational programs for the deaf on the lives of the deaf. Here, it is sufficient to note that hearing people have traditionally been in almost total control of those programs.

The deaf began to be viewed by the hearing as an unfortunate and dependent group of people, and not solely as incapable of thinking. This view led the hearing "charitably" to make exceptions for the deaf. In the 1870s, several states enacted stringent laws for the repression of tramps and beggars, but excepted "various unfortunate classes of humanity," among which were the deaf (Fay, 1879: 194). In the same spirit, deaf children have at times been allowed to ride the railroad for free, and deaf adults have been exempted from certain types of state taxes. More recently, two social scientists noticed that police officers are often reluctant to arrest the deaf because they already have one "strike" against them, their deafness (Furfey and Harte, 1968).

When not seen as totally incompetent or as dependent, the deaf have been excluded from various activities because it has been assumed that the ability to hear is necessary for such activities. This is a prevalent attitude today. Traditionally, the deaf have had difficulty obtaining a driver's license, though the situation has improved greatly in the past several decades (Crammatte, 1970; Grant, 1970). When the deaf have been involved in accidents, deafness has often been presumed to constitute negligence; at times, these accidents have given rise to serious debate as to whether the deaf should be allowed to continue to drive (Gruss, 1940, 1941). As a result, the deaf have had difficulty obtaining automobile insurance (as well as other forms of insurance) at a reasonable rate (Crammatte, 1970). Consequently, an insurance company which is run by and for the deaf and was established in 1901 flourishes. All of this was based on the assumption that hearing was necessary for competent driving. Research indicates, though, that the deaf have no higher—and may have lower accident rates than does the general public (Schein, 1968).

With respect to employment, the deaf have been unemployed, underemployed, and likely to be passed over for promotion. Advancement usually ceases when a supervisory position is approached because the deaf are believed to be lacking the "essential" skill necessary for such positions. They cannot use the telephone. Hearing workers who have been trained by the deaf are frequently promoted over those same deaf people into supervisory positions (Jones, 1969; Craig and Collins, 1970). In the past, the Civil Service classified the deaf with the insane as persons barred from examination. Routinely, the Civil Service has issued standard statements that the ability to hear conversational speech with or without a hearing aid is a requirement for various jobs, without actually determining whether normal hearing is necessary for the successful performance of those jobs (Bowe et al., 1973). Even educators of the deaf have promoted the idea that the deaf should be satisfied with trade skills and not aspire to higher education (Schein, 1968: 96).

The point of the brief history which I presented is not just that the hearing have treated the deaf unfairly or even inhumanely. They have. The point is not even that the hearing have largely misunderstood the deaf. They have done that too. The important point is that, based on various ideas about what it means to be deaf, the hearing have created a world in which the deaf live but are not fully part of. The bases of that historical relationship continue today. The deaf remain outsiders in a hearing world, and their lives can only be fully understood with that in mind.

A "sociological imagination" requires us to locate deaf people within the wider social structure, within the hearing world (Mills, 1959). That imagination enables us to see how the personal troubles of individual deaf people are often the reflection and outcome of their status as outsiders in a hearing world.

Deaf people, though, are not alone in their status as

outsiders. Many groups of people have had to contend with a world which was largely created and now is controlled by someone else. The poor have had to deal with a world run by those who are not poor. The disabled are outsiders in a nondisabled world. Barry Adam (1978) speaks of blacks, Jews, and gays as "inferiorized" people. By that he does not mean that they are inherently inferior rather, that they have been put and kept in an inferior position. Blacks are outsiders in a world where color matters a great deal. Jews are outsiders in a gentile world. Homosexuals must contend with a heterosexual world that often finds their behavior disgusting. To various degrees, these people have been exterminated, lynched, arrested, and rejected. In popular stereotypes they are portrayed in various negative ways: greedy, foul-smelling, shiftless, brutish, flashy, loud, effeminate, and so on. Each group of outsiders faces unique situations arising from the particular reasons that they are outsiders. They also may face many similar problems and consequently develop similar solutions. It is quite interesting that people's attitudes toward the deaf and toward the blind are related to their attitudes toward minority groups and blacks. People who have negative feelings toward one outsider group are likely to have negative feelings toward other outsider groups (Cowen et al., 1958, 1967). Not only have the deaf been historically viewed as unable to think, but, as Adam (1978: 50) notes, "scientific studies have repeatedly attempted to link low intelligence with inferiorized groups."

Therefore, understanding the deaf as outsiders in a hearing world increases our understanding of other outsiders as well. Further, drawing on the experiences and situations of other outsiders is likely to help us understand the deaf. Throughout the following chapters, then, I will draw on works about black Americans, gays, the disabled, and other outsiders in order better to understand the deaf.

Each of these outsiders faces a reality which has largely been created and dominated by someone else. And as McCall and Simmons (1966: 42) note:

Reality, then, in this distinctively human world, is not a hard immutable thing but is fragile and adjudicated a thing to be debated, compromised, and legislated. Those who most succeed in this world are those who are most persuasive and effective in having their interpretations ratified as true reality. Those who do not are relegated to the fringes of the human world, are executed as heretics or traitors, ridiculed as crackpots, or locked up as lunatics.

They also become outsiders in that world.

DEAFNESS

In everyday terms, deafness often means "stone deaf." However, there are relatively few people who have no sense of hearing. Among professionals in the field, defining and determining deafness is a complicated matter.

People are born with or acquire various types and degrees of hearing impairments. Hearing impairments vary according to many factors: Chronicity (whether the impairment is temporary or not), age of onset, degree and type of loss, and cause are just some (Schein, 1968). Hearing impairments have been classified in various ways. They have been classified according to the amount of functional hearing which is left, the degree of loss in the speech range, the amount of speech and language handicap which is a consequence of the loss, educational requirements, and so on (Levine, 1960). Any criteria for defining deafness will necessarily be arbitrary.

A long-standing and often quoted definition, established in 1937 by the Conference of Executives of American Schools for the Deaf, states that the deaf are "those in whom the sense of hearing is non-functional for the ordinary purposes of life" (Stevenson et al., 1938: 3). Two difficulties exist with this definition. First, what are the ordinary purposes of life for which hearing should be functional? Presumably one would like to be able to hear spoken conversation. Consequently, the inability to hear and understand speech is often used as a basis for defining deafness. Yet, what about hearing a police siren, an alarm clock, or some other sound? Second, it is often extremely difficult to specify when functional hearing shades into nonfunctional hearing because hearing ability is continuous (Barker et al., 1953: 191). Because hearing losses are vastly complex, audiological examinations are typically used to determine the nature of the loss. In order to understand audiological examinations and their results, the nature of sound must be understood.[3] Sound has both physical and psychological attributes. Physically, sound varies according to frequency, intensity, and complexity. The complementary psychological characteristics are pitch, loudness, and timbre.

Frequency refers to the number of cycles per second (cps), that a particle of the sound wave completes. People can auditorily respond to frequencies which range from 20 to 20,000 cps. They respond with greatest facility to frequencies from 500 to 4000 cps. Human speech ranges from 250 to 4000 cps with most speech sounds falling between 500 and 2000 cps. Thus people typically respond with greatest sensitivity at the frequency range essential for hearing speech. Listeners will typically judge high frequency sounds as high in pitch and low frequency sounds as low in pitch.

Intensity refers to the power or energy of the sound. It is measured in bels, a unit named after Alexander Graham Bell. Bels express the extent to which one sound intensity is greater than another. Bels are a logarithmic unit (to the base 10). Thus, a sound which measures 1 bel more than another is 10 times as intense. A sound 2 bels as intense would be 100 times as intense. A sound 3 bels as intense would be 1000 times as intense, and so on. In order to make finer distinctions, the decibel (db), which is one-tenth of a bel, is used.

Because the decibel is a ratio, a standard reference level against which other sounds are compared is used. The standard reference level is approximately the intensity of the faintest sound that can be heard by the best ear. A sound measured at 10 decibels would be 10 times as intense as this faintest sound. A whisper has an intensity of about 15 to 25 decibels. Conversational speech is between 50 and 65 decibels. Traffic noise is 75 to 85 decibels. The noise of a hair dryer measures about 80 decibels; that of a power lawn mower, about 110 decibels; and that of a jet airplane 100 feet away, approximately 140 decibels. Sounds of high intensity are likely to be psychologically perceived as loud. Those of low intensity will be called soft. Loudness also varies on the basis of frequency. Further, it varies from person to person. What is loud to one person may not be to another. Witness the generational gap over the question of the loudness of much popular music.

Complexity refers to the fact that most sounds in our everyday lives are a mixture of frequencies and intensities. Psychologically we perceive that mixture as timbre. It is through complexity and its psychological complement, timbre, that we can distinquish sounds which are quite similar—for example, human voices.

Put very simply, audiological examinations determine how intense sound must be at different frequencies in order for an individual to hear the sound. The frequencies of the speech range are of greatest importance. Hearing impairments are often such that, depending on the frequency of the sound, different intensities are necessary in order for the sound to be heard. In other words, a hearing-impaired person may hear sounds of low frequency better than those of high frequency, or vice versa. Patterns of hearing losses can be very complex, and they often differ between the right and left ear. The detailed pattern is charted on an audiogram. To simplify this complexity, the average hearing loss over the frequencies of the speech range for the better ear, the BEA, is often taken as a gross indication of the individual's hearing loss. For example, someone with a BEA of 80 decibels could not hear ordinary conversation, but perhaps could faintly hear people shouting. A hearing loss of 10 to 25 decibels might be classified as normal; 25 to 40 decibels would be slight; 40 to 55 decibels would be mild to moderate; 55 to 70 decibels could be termed moderately severe; a 70 to 90 decibel loss is severe; and over 90 decibels is profound (Mindel and Vernon, 1971: 33). Depending on the nature and type of the hearing loss, a hearing aid may or may not appreciably improve the hearing-impaired individual's hearing.

Hearing impairments are extremely complex. They differ enormously from person to person. Therefore, little agreement exists on what should be the audiological criteria for defining deafness. Some have suggested that only those whose hearing impairment is 82 decibels or worse within the speech range should be termed deaf. Others have put that limit as low as 15 decibels (Schein, 1968).

Abstract audiological criteria will not help us much, however, in understanding the deaf as outsiders in a hearing world. As I explain in the following chapter, there are many people who are profoundly hearing-impaired who are not socially deaf, who are not members of deaf communities. Conversely, there are many socially deaf people, members of deaf communities, who are not profoundly hearing-impaired. Some members of the deaf community can use the telephone reasonably well. Those hearing-impaired people who become members of deaf communities are typically educated in particular educational programs for the deaf. Whether they are educated in those programs or not is only partially related to audiological criteria. It is also related to successful recognition of the hearing loss, parental desires, the availability of other programs, and so on. Thus, audiological criteria provide only an incomplete beginning for understanding outsiders in a hearing world.

The age of onset of the hearing loss, however, deserves special mention. It is an important factor for several reasons. First, in general, the earlier that children become deaf, the greater difficulty they will have learning to speak and develop language skills. Those who are born deaf or who lose their hearing before the age of two or three are called prelingually deaf. Children typically learn to speak and develop their language abilities through hearing the talk of others around them. The development of speech and language is not merely an imitative process, though. It depends on infants and young children actively manipulating what they hear (and utter themselves) and having those manipulations modified by feedback from the environment. Infants and young children who are deaf, however, received little meaningful oral input or feedback from their environment. Poor speech, of course, has consequences for how the deaf interact with the hearing. Language difficulties often lead to poor academic development. Deaf children typically score several years behind their hearing counterparts on academic achievement tests (Trybus and Karchmer, 1977). Educational programs for deaf children, of course, are designed to develop their speech, language, and academic skills. The philosophies of those programs have played an important part in the social world of the deaf. Second, those who lose their hearing after adolescence are unlikely to become members of deaf communities. In large part, they do not become members because they do not share the experiences of those who are born deaf or who lose their hearing in childhood. And in part, those experiences involve being educated in special programs for the deaf. These points will be taken up in more detail in the next chapter.

Estimates of the prevalence of deafness in the United States are bound to vary because of the inconsistency in defining and measuring deafness. The U.S. Bureau of the Census's figures have fluctuated from 67.5 per 100,000 in 1880 to 32.1 per 100,000 in 1900 (Schein and Delk, 1974: 17). Due to such fluctuations, the Bureau ceased enumerating the deaf after 1930. The most recent census of the deaf, conducted in 1971 by New York University, found that hearing impairment is the most prevalent chronic physical impairment in the United States. More than 13 million people have some form of hearing impairment. Almost 2 million people are deaf. They cannot hear and understand speech. Those who suffered early profound hearing losses (before the end of adolescence) are a smaller group. Approximately 410,000 people are "prevocationally" deaf—at a rate of 203 per 100,000 (Schein and Delk, 1974).[4] In the Chicago area, the location of my research, there are an estimated 12,000 deaf men, women, and children (The Deaf Lutheran, 1974).[5] While most deaf people are outsiders in a hearing world, members of the deaf community predominantly come from the "prevocationally" deaf, and perhaps even more so from those who lost their hearing before adolescence. It is to the deaf community that I turn my attention now.

NOTES

1. This brief historical section draws heavily from the following works: Gruss (1940, 1941), Best (1943), Bender (1970), and Boese (1971).

2. See Furth (1966, 1971) and Vernon (1967) for a review of the research which indicates that thinking depends very little on linguistic ability. It is not the medium through which thinking takes place. Symbols are necessary, though, for thinking which is concerned with events that are not perceptually present.

3. This discussion of sound and of deafness is based on Davis and Silverman (1960), Myklebust (1964), and Mindel and Vernon (1971).

4. The prevocationally deaf were defined as those "who could not hear and understand speech and who had lost (or never had) that ability prior to 19 years of age" (Schein and Delk, 1974: 2). Age was not a limitation for assessing the general prevalence of hearing impairments and deafness in the population. The definition of deafness was operationalized through a seven-item Guttman-type hearing scale which asked respondents to indicate which types of sounds they could hear.

5. Using the U.S. Bureau of the Census (1976) estimates of the population for the Chicago SMSA (standard metropolitan statistical area) and for Cook County and the rate of 203 per 100,000 "prevocationally" deaf individuals in the United States, I estimate that there are approximately 14,000 deaf men, women, and children in the Chicago SMSA, and 11,000 in Cook County.

2

THE DEAF COMMUNITY

Outsiders deal with their fate as outsiders in various ways. Some desire to shed their status as outsiders. They seek to become as much like those who create and control the world as possible. A disfigured man has plastic surgery. Immigrants shorten their names and leave the "old world" ways behind. An overweight individual goes to a reducing clinic. A criminal goes straight. A light-skinned black passes for white. If successful, these people are no longer outsiders, though they may have to deal with their past lives as outsiders.

Some outsiders go it alone. They live on the fringes of social life. They form few attachments among the world of outsiders. They feel uneasy or are not welcomed with the larger social world. The closet gay shuts himself off from both the straight and the gay worlds. Some alcoholics are shunned by sober society, but they seek no help from Alcoholics Anonymous and find no comfort among skid row society. Some hearing-impaired people are caught between the hearing and the deaf worlds. These outsiders bear their burdens by themselves.

Others, though, form organized groups. The members are those who share a similar fate. Many are self-help groups like

Alcoholics Anonymous or Little People of America (Sagarin, 1969). These organizations serve several purposes. They may seek to control or eliminate that which led to its members becoming outsiders in the first place. Thus, Alcoholics Anonymous attempts to keep its members abstinent, and weight loss groups try to have their members control their eating (Laslett and Warren, 1975). Other groups seek to increase knowledge about their situation and spread that knowledge to the general public. Some lobby for favorable legislation. Others have a social purpose. They function as dating and mating services. Fellow outsiders can become acquainted, make friends, and even find future spouses (Weinberg, 1968). While important, these organizations are typically narrow in their focus. They occupy only a small amount of the members' time and commitment.

Some outsiders create and maintain communities. They may live among those who are similarly slighted by the wider society. Blacks may inhabit urban ghettos. Some Spanish Americans live in barrios. Polish Americans may reside in ethnic neighborhoods. Their neighbors are fellow outsiders. These communities are bounded by streets, railroad tracks, and rivers. At least in part, these communities are spatially located.

Other outsiders form communities which cannot be as easily outlined on a map. These communities are only loosely tied to any particular area of the city. While members of some of these communities may reside predominantly in certain parts of the city—for example, in some large cities there are "gay ghettos" (Levine, 1979)—most of these communities have members scattered throughout the city. These communities do not consist of street addresses. Instead, they are created through friendships, informal acquaintances, marriages, clubs, bars, publications, religious organizations, and so on. Gays create such communities (Warren, 1974). Outsiders in a hearing world do, too.

Communities of outsiders are likely to have a profound impact on their members' lives. As Becker (1963: 38) notes

of members of deviant groups (and all we need to do is
substitute "outsider" for "deviant"):

> Members of organized deviant groups of course have one thing in
> common: their deviance. It gives them a sense of common
> fate. . . . From a sense of common fate, from having to face the
> same problems, grows a deviant subculture: a set of perspectives
> and understandings about what the world is like and how to deal
> with it, and a set of routine activities based on those perspectives.
> Membership in such a group solidifies a deviant identity.

In this chapter I explore three aspects of deaf communities: membership, social organization, and national networks
(the social bonds which tie together widely dispersed deaf
people). Membership is not a matter of birthright. Most who
are deaf are not members of deaf communities. Among those
who are members, however, distinctions are likely to develop.
Members use those distinctions in organizing their relationships with one another. Finally, a national network of relationships may be developed which ties together deaf people
who are dispersed throughout the country. In fact, through
sharing a common fate, a sense of solidarity may be created
among deaf people who are otherwise complete strangers.
These three aspects are interrelated. They are all an outgrowth of the deaf's status as outsiders in a hearing world.

COMMUNITY

Sociologists are fond of applying the term "community"
to various types of social arrangements. Towns, villages, and
cities are somewhat obviously and commonsensically called
communities. But there are also prison communities and
religious communities. Even factories, trade unions, and corporations have been referred to as communities (Minar and
Greer, 1969). Understandably, this confusion has led Dennis
Poplin (1972: 3) to lament that the term "community" falls
into that category of words, used daily by the sociologist,
which "take on so many shades of meaning that it is difficult
to endow them with scientific precision."

While there is not complete agreement, most sociologists
are in basic agreement that communities consist of people in
"social interaction within a geographic area and having one or
more additional common ties" (Hillery, 1955: 111). This
description broadly characterizes deaf communities.

MEMBERSHIP

Deafness is not a sufficient condition for membership in
deaf communities, though some degree of hearing impairment is a necessary condition, which I examine later. Deafness does not make "its members part of a natural community" (Furth, 1973: 2). Membership in a deaf community must
be *achieved*; it is not an ascribed status (Markowicz and
Woodward, 1978). Membership in a deaf community is
achieved through (1) *identification* with the deaf world, (2)
shared experiences that come of being hearing impaired, and
(3) *participation* in the community's activities.[1] Without all
three characteristics, one cannot be nor would one choose to
be a member of a deaf community.

IDENTIFICATION

A deaf community is in part a "moral" phenomenon. It
involves a "sense of identity and unity with one's group and a
feeling of involvement and wholeness on the part of the
individual" (Poplin, 1972: 7).

A deaf woman, hearing-impaired since childhood, dramatically described her realization in her late teens and early
twenties that she was part of the deaf world:

> I didn't think I was very deaf myself. But when I saw these
> people (at a deaf organization) I knew I belonged to their world. I
> didn't belong to the hearing world. Once you are deaf, you are
> deaf, period. If you put something black in white paint, you can't
> get the black out. Same with the deaf. Once you are deaf, you're
> always deaf.

While it is problematic both physiologically and in terms of identification that "once you are deaf, you are always deaf," the woman's remarks express her commitment to the deaf world.[2] Whether members dramatically realize it or not, what is important is their commitment to and identification with the deaf. Other members, who attended schools and classes for the deaf since childhood and continued their interaction in the deaf world as adults, may, upon looking back, find no dramatic moment when they realized that they had become part of a deaf community.

Members of the deaf community feel more comfortable with deaf people than they do with the hearing. They feel a sense of belonging. A young deaf woman explained:

> At a club for the deaf, if I see a deaf person whom I don't know, I will go up to that person and say, "Hi! What's your name?" I would never do that to a hearing person.

Again, when I asked a deaf couple how they felt about hearing people,

> the wife answered that she likes to be with her *own* people. According to her husband, though, she can get along well with the hearing. Her speech is understandable, and her husband feels that she is a good lipreader. He recalled that one day he was across the street conversing with a neighbor, but could not understand him. His wife, looking through the window, did.

Most deaf individuals cannot lipread that well—nor, probably, can this wife on most occasions. As she said herself, the neighbor's speech seemed so clear that time. What is important, though, is her desire to be with her *own* people. This identification with other deaf people is the foundation for membership in the deaf community. Based on this identification, members of a Jewish synagogue for the deaf donated items to a bazaar run by a Lutheran church for the deaf, rather than to a synagogue for hearing Jews.

Identification with the deaf world can momentarily unite people who are otherwise complete strangers. Deaf Americans who travel abroad are often cordially received by members of deaf clubs in foreign countries. While my hearing companions and I were traveling on the subway in Paris, a group of deaf Japanese tourists noticed that we were signing to one another. When it is noisy, signing often comes in handy. While we had difficulty communicating with one another due to the (sign) language barrier, the deaf Japanese tourists were quite obviously pleased to meet some American people who they thought were deaf. (They never did realize that we were able to hear.)

Not all deaf or hearing-impaired people, though, identify with the deaf world. Those who lost their hearing later in life through an accident, occupational hazard, or presbycusis (i.e., the aging process) do not seek to become members of deaf communities.[3] Rather, as Goffman (1963) notes, they are likely to stigmatize members of deaf communities in the same way that those with normal hearing stigmatize them. Others, impaired from birth or from an early age, may never have developed such an identification. They are likely to have had hearing parents and were educated in schools for the hearing or in oral schools for the deaf (which I will discuss later). Some may participate in activities of deaf communities, but are not members. They are tolerated, though they are not accepted, by the members. While audiologically they are deaf, socially they are not.

A hearing-impaired man, who participates in a religious organization for the deaf but is not part of the deaf community, explained his self-identity in the following way:

> In everyday life I consider myself a hearing person. [His hearing-impaired wife interjected that she did too.] I usually forget it that I have a hearing problem. Sometimes I'm so lost [absorbed] in the hearing world, I mean I don't even realize I have a hearing problem. It seems automatic. I don't know what it is. I feel I'm hearing people to the deaf and hearing. I don't feel hearing-impaired not even if I have a hard time to understand somebody. Still I don't feel I'm deaf because I couldn't hear you or understand you.

The same man remarked:

I was deaf for a few days. My ears blocked up. That was [a] scary
moment for me. I was completely deaf. I was walking and it was
completely quiet. I tried talking on the phone. I used my ampli-
fier all the way up. It didn't work too much. And I was deaf. My
wife used to call me and I didn't hear her call me. Nothing! I
could talk and that's why I was still hearing. I could talk even if I
couldn't hear a thing.

Hearing-impaired people like this man and his wife are
often a source of both ill feelings and amusement for members of deaf communities. They are a source of ill feelings
because their behavior does not respect the identity of the
deaf community. Thus, this same hearing-impaired man was
severely criticized for having someone at a board meeting of a
religious group interpret his spoken remarks into sign language, rather than signing himself. His failure to sign was
interpreted as insult to the members of the deaf community
who served on the board. As I explain later, signing skill and
communication preference are indications of one's commitment to the deaf community. Those who are opposed to
signing or who do not sign are not members of the community.

They are a source of amusement for trying to be what
members of deaf communities feel they are not, hearing. A
deaf couple were both critical and amused at the attempt of
the same hearing-impaired man's wife to hide her deafness.
As they explained:

A hearing woman who signs well came up to her [the wife] at a
religious gathering, and assuming that she was deaf, which she is,
began to sign to her. The wife became flustered, put her own
hands down and started talking.

Such hearing-impaired people serve as examples that members of deaf communities use in explaining to others what
their community is like and in reaffirming to themselves who
they are. These hearing-impaired people help to define for

the members the boundary of their community and their identity as deaf people. The members reject the feelings of these "misguided" hearing-impaired people—feelings which deny their deafness. And in rejection, the members affirm who they are and what their community is.

SHARED EXPERIENCES

In developing an identification with the deaf world, members of deaf communities share many similar experiences. These experiences relate particularly to the everyday problems of navigating in a hearing world and to being educated in special programs for the deaf. In Chapters 5 and 6 I examine in detail the everyday problems of stigmatization and communication that the deaf face when they encounter the hearing.

Since childhood, members of deaf communities have experienced repeated frustration in making themselves understood, embarrassing misunderstandings, and the loneliness of being left out by family, neighborhood acquaintances, and others. Such past and present experiences help to strengthen a deaf person's identification with the deaf world. A *typical* instance of these experiences, remarkable only because it is so routine, was described by a deaf man who speaks well:

Most of my friends are deaf. I feel more comfortable with them. Well, we have the same feelings. We are more comfortable with each other. I can communicate good with hearing people, but in a group, no. For example, I go bowling. Have a league of hearing bowlers. Four of them will be talking, talking, talking and I will be left out. Maybe if there was one person I would catch some by lipreading, but the conversation passes back and forth so quickly. I can't keep up. I just let it go; pay attention to my bowling. Many things like that.

Or as the same deaf man explained when I asked him during an interview, two months later, "What are your feelings about hearing people?":

Well, funny. With my good speech and lipreading ability I don't
care to mix with hearing people. I've been deaf all my life. But I
never feel comfortable with hearing people. I could if it's a
one-to-one basis, but in a group I'm out. And I don't want to be
put in a situation, an embarrassing situation [where] I don't feel
comfortable. That's why I don't do it.

I went on, "You told me once you went bowling with
hearing people. How was it? Did you feel included?" His
response was:

No. No. I enjoy bowling with the deaf more, even though most of
them are [pause] not on my level, my intellectual level, I mean.
They have ability, but were never given a chance to learn. So I
never give them any feeling that I am superior to them.

What comes through so clearly in this man's remarks is a
mixture of his feelings of belonging with fellow members of
the deaf community and the uneasiness of interacting with
the hearing. That uneasiness, which is part of the shared
experiences of being deaf, is a basis for identification with
the deaf world as well as a factor which further strengthens
identification with the deaf world.

However, to be a member of a deaf community one need
not actually be deaf. Some members have lesser degrees of
hearing impairment. As children, though, they were pro-
cessed through educational programs for the deaf. These
children were not necessarily mislabeled, though certainly
some were. Rather, many times no local programs for "hard
of hearing" children or children with less severe impairments
were available. Children with various degrees of impairment,
ranging from mild to profound, were educated together.
Nowadays more specialized educational programs exist, but,
still, children with widely varying hearing losses are educated
(often properly so) in the same program. Through such
processing, these children developed friendships with deaf
children and an identification with the deaf. As adults, they
moved comfortably into deaf communities. With amplification, these members of deaf communities are often able to

use the telephone successfully, if somewhat haltingly. Some converse with hearing people reasonably well. Yet, due to that childhood processing in programs for the deaf, these hearing-impaired people choose to live their lives within deaf communities. Audiologically they are not deaf; socially they are (Furfey and Harte, 1964, 1968; Schein, 1968).

Other members of a deaf community may have once been deaf, but through surgery or fortuitous circumstances they have regained some hearing. Though no longer severely hearing-impaired, they remain active in the deaf community where their identity as a person developed. A dramatic case is that of a now slightly hearing-impaired man. He went to the state school for the deaf in Illinois. His childhood friends were deaf. During World War II, though, he regained much of his hearing from working in a munitions plant. The loud blasts from testing the bombs apparently improved his hearing. Consequently, his speech also improved. Only his modest hearing aid indicates that he has a slight impairment. However, his wife is deaf, most of their friends are deaf, and he is active in a state organization for the deaf. When I asked, "As your speech got better, did you continue to associate with your deaf friends in . . . [town]?" he explained:

> Oh, yeh, I'm more involved with the deaf community now than I was back then [during World War II]. To me they are still my family. I feel more at home when I walk into a room with 1000 deaf people more so than walking into a room with 1000 hearing people, nondeaf. I feel at home. I can relate to them. We had something in common—our childhood, our education, our problems, and all that.

That communality of experience and identity is the basis for belonging to the deaf community. Some who are audiologically deaf lack it. Others who are no longer deaf or never were profoundly hearing-impaired possess it. Without it, one cannot be nor would one choose to be a member of the deaf community.[4]

Since membership in deaf communities is based on shared experiences of being deaf and identification with the deaf world, it is difficult for hearing individuals to be members of such communities. In general, those who are not outsiders are unlikely to be members of communities of outsiders. Though it is not impossible, heterosexuals are unlikely to be members of the gay community and whites are unlikely to be members of the black community (Warren, 1974: 150-151). A deaf woman put it simply: "Hearing people are lost in the deaf world, just as deaf people are lost in the hearing world." Another deaf woman, married to a hearing man whom I have met and who signs quite well, explained:

> Even though my husband signs well enough to communicate with the deaf, he isn't really comfortable among them. Some of my friends accept him. Others, who don't know him as well, don't. At a club he might be signing, and some deaf don't know that he is hearing. When they learn that he is hearing and that he is my husband, they say, "Good! You sign well." But he doesn't really feel comfortable with the deaf. I wonder how a hearing person could feel comfortable.

Hearing people, as indicated by these two deaf women and by other members of the community, are not part of the deaf community. Marrying a deaf individual is not sufficient for obtaining membership in the community. Again and again I was told by deaf respondents that they knew of no hearing people who were members of the community, though specific hearing people that they knew from work or childhood might be their friends.

Two hearing women, one with a deaf daughter and the other with a deaf sister, were pointed out to me by some deaf Jews as active participants in religious and social functions of deaf Jews. They seemed to be accepted within this more limited group of deaf people. Yet neither one claimed to be members of the community. They were friends, particularly of some deaf Jews, but they were not members. One of the women noted that when deaf people who do not know her learn that she is hearing, they immediately slow their signing to her. Some deaf, when signing to hearing people, switch to signed English rather than use American Sign Language (Markowicz and Woodward, 1978). As I mention later in this chapter, signed English is used in formal occasions, whereas American Sign Language is used among fellow members of the deaf community. Maneuvers like these by the deaf are an indication that the hearing person is not fully one of them. Outsiders are often wary and resentful of those from the dominant world—blacks of whites, gays of straights, and so on. Likewise, deaf people are skeptical of hearing people's motives and intentions. A deaf man remarked: "When a hearing person starts to associate with the deaf, the deaf begin to wonder why that hearing person is here. What does that hearing person want?" When a "hard of hearing" woman, who for years had associated exclusively with the hearing, started a North Shore club for the deaf, her motives and behavior were questioned by some of the deaf members. I was warned myself by two deaf leaders to expect such skepticism and resistance by members of the deaf community. I encountered little in my research, but having deaf parents and clearly establishing my intentions probably allayed members' suspicions.

Outsider communities, though, may grant courtesy membership to "wise" people who are not similarly stigmatized (Goffman, 1963). These individuals are "normal," yet they are familiar with and sympathetic to the conditions of outsiders. For example, gay communities grant courtesy membership to "wise" heterosexuals: heterosexual couples or single females known as "fag hags" (Warren, 1974: 113). Researchers are often granted that status. Yet that courtesy membership represents only a partial acceptance by the outsiders of the "normals."

Some hearing individuals are courtesy members of deaf communities. They may be educators, counselors, interpreters, or friends of the deaf. Often they have deafness in their families: deaf parents, siblings, children, or even spouses. Yet their membership is just that, a courtesy, which recognizes the fundamental fact that no matter how empathic they are, no matter that there is deafness in their families, they are not deaf and can never "really" know what it means to be deaf.

PARTICIPATION

Active participation in the deaf community is the final criteria for being a member. Participation, though, is an outgrowth of identification with the deaf world and of sharing similar experiences of being hearing-impaired. In that respect, then, it is the least important characteristic for being a member of the deaf community. Yet the deaf community is not merely a symbolic community of hearing-impaired people who share similar experiences. It is also created through marriages, friendships, acquaintances, parties, clubs, religious organizations, and published materials. The activities provide the body of the community, whereas the identification and shared experiences provide the soul.

Thus, a deaf couple, who lived in the Chicago area for years, were not warmly received when they began to attend a deaf, Protestant congregation. The members of the congregation wondered where they had been all these years. Members interpreted their lack of participation as a lack of identification with themselves and a lack of commitment to the deaf community.

Participation, however, varies among the members of deaf communities. Involvement in community activities is tempered by outside commitments concerned with work and family, and travel to and from activities, as well as individual preference. More importantly, what activities one participates in and with whom one associates help to organize relationships among members of the deaf community.

Membership in deaf communities is thus based on identification with the deaf, shared experiences of being hearing-impaired, and participation in the activities of the community. As a deaf woman stated:

> To be part of the deaf community you have to associate with the deaf all the time. (Have to depend on the deaf for social activities?) Not only social, any part of your everyday life. Then you can become part (of the community).

Membership is a matter of commitment.

SOCIAL ORGANIZATION

While the larger social world may often treat outsiders as a homogeneous group, the outsiders themselves create distinctions within their group. Gays distinguish among "elite," "career," and "deviant" gays (Warren, 1972). Lower-class blacks may vilify middle-class blacks for being Uncle Toms (Pettigrew, 1964). The deaf community, too, is heterogeneous. Through differential participation with other members and in various activities of the deaf community, members organize their relationships with one another.

Outsiders, whether they be deaf or not, live within a larger world. Some are not born as outsiders, but only later acquire that status. All are socialized to some degree within the dominant culture. Consequently, communities of outsiders and their subcultures are continuous with the dominant culture of the larger society (Plummer, 1975: 157). Therefore, it is not surprising that some characteristics which members of the dominant culture use to differentiate among themselves are also used by members of communities of outsiders. For example, social class and race are important characteristics which differentiate members of male gay communities (Warren, 1974). Members of the deaf community use several differentiators in organizing relationships with one another which are also used in the hearing world.

Among the deaf, race, sophistication as indirectly indicated by educational attainment (as well as educational attainment itself), and age seem to be the most important. While social class, sex, and religious affiliation have some impact on the social organization of the deaf community, they are less important for understanding the community than are the three characteristics first mentioned.

Social class seems to be relatively unimportant within the deaf community. In one sense it is related to and thus operates through sophistication and education. More significantly, however, class is not one of the important attributes which deaf people use in establishing relations with one another. The reasons have little to do with egalitarian motives of the deaf community. The range of social class within the deaf community is truncated. While there are many who are lower class, working class, lower-middle class, or middle class, there are few who are upper-middle or upper class. One usually must be a professional, a doctor or lawyer for example, or a successful businessman to attain upper-middle-class or upper-class status. Compared to the hearing, relatively few deaf people become professionals or obtain other high status jobs (Schein and Delk, 1974). Consequently, social class is not as important in determining relationships among the deaf as it seems to be within the dominant society. This does not mean that class distinctions are not made among the deaf, but rather that such distinctions do not explain much of the differentiation among the deaf.

As in most communities, sex is used to organize relationships among members of the deaf community. A fraternal organization of the deaf has separate men's and women's groups. Women form coffee clubs and go to bridal showers. Men have poker clubs. Yet sex is less important than other factors for understanding the deaf community. The same is true with religion. While members of the deaf community worship in different ways and some not at all, religion is not a decisive factor in differentiating members of the community. While religious teachings are important to some members, for many, worship is primarily a social gathering. Which church one attends often depends on where one's friends go and whether the minister can sign or not. Consequently, I will not examine sex or religious differentiation here.

Other characteristics which members of an outsider community use to organize their relationships with one another are related to their unique position within the dominant world. For example, within the black community skin color has played an important but diminishing role (Udry et al., 1971). Within the deaf community, communication preference and skill, the relative emphasis that members give to signing and speaking, is an important basis on which relationships are organized. I will examine this characteristic closely, because it is crucial for understanding the deaf community in

a hearing world. First, though, I will examine race, sophistication, and age, characteristics which differentiate members of
the deaf community much as they do those who are part of
the hearing world.

Race

Race is an important characteristic among outsiders as well
as among those who are not outsiders. Among gays, there are
all-black, all-white, and all-Chicano communities (Warren,
1974: 88). Similarly, separate white and black deaf communities exist in the Chicago area. Interaction between white and
black deaf is minimal. Clubs for the deaf are often highly
segregated, either by choice or subtle persuasion (Anderson
and Bowe, 1972). A senior citizens' club for the deaf has no
black members. None have applied, though they are welcome, the president of the club informed me. A deaf black
woman did attend its meetings, but only after I visited her
and suggested that she do so. She had never attended the
meetings before, though she had participated in some of the
outings and activities sponsored by the club.

A well-known social club for the deaf in Chicago only
recently changed its policy to permit blacks to become members. According to the secretary of the club, the membership
policy became "flexible" about four years ago when the club
began sponsoring a basketball team. Blacks are permitted to
join the team. Presently, out of more than 200 members,
though, the club has only 9 who are black. Using census
figures for 1970 (U.S. Bureau of the Census, 1973) and rates
of deafness for blacks and whites (Schein and Delk, 1974:
32), I have estimated that for the Chicago metropolitan area,
14% of the deaf population is black; for just the city of
Chicago, 32% of the deaf population is black. However, 9
black members out of more than 200 is less than 4.5% of the
club's membership. On a typical weekend night when the
club is open, 2 or 3 out of 50 or 60 in attendance may be
black. It seems that athletics are where black and white deaf
are most likely to come together.

The club itself has recently moved from downtown to the north side of the city. The downtown area was a dangerous location with its poor lighting, little pedestrian traffic, and all too frequent muggings. Equally important to some white deaf was that too many black deaf, many who worked at the downtown post office, were coming to the club. This happened especially on Bank Night, one Saturday each month where cash prizes could be won. Since the club has been moved, fewer blacks are coming, which meets with the approval of many white deaf. And, as some white deaf told me, the blacks have their own club on the south side, though nobody seems to be sure when, where, or if it still meets.

The state organization for the deaf, the IAD (Illinois Association of the Deaf), is also primarily composed of white members. While no precise figures are available, the president estimated that perhaps 50 of the approximately 800 members are black.[5] As a past president explained:

We have a few black deaf [in the state organization]. But not as many as we'd like to have. The black deaf live by themselves.

The black deaf in Chicago do live by themselves, primarily on the south and west side of the city, as do the blacks who hear. The white deaf, along with the whites who hear, tend to live on the north and northwest sides and in the suburbs. Geographically, the white and black deaf are separated, as are their hearing counterparts. Further, as a deaconess for a black congregation explained, the black deaf in her church will not risk their lives on the El (the subway) at night to go to the social club for deaf on the north side.

Geographical separation between black and white deaf is not the only reason for distinct black and white deaf communities. Since white deaf adults grow up in the larger society where there is prejudice, it would be naive to expect that none were prejudiced themselves. Some white deaf have remarked that the black deaf were just like them—they are both deaf. Similarly, white gays may characterize black gays as similar to themselves (Warren, 1974: 89-90). However,

other deaf individuals have indicated that they neither understand nor desire to interact with the black deaf. A minister to
a white deaf congregation explained that he could not convince his white members who live on the south and southwest
sides to go to a closer congregation which serves the black
deaf. A young deaf man explained:

> He isn't a member of the north side club for the deaf. He went a
> few times, but didn't enjoy himself because so many blacks went.
> When I told him that the club had moved to a new location, he
> replied that blacks still go there in large numbers. However, he
> isn't against blacks. He can enjoy being with black deaf if they
> respect white people.

Other white members of the deaf community complain
that the black deaf fight or cause trouble at the club, though
some realize that white deaf do too. That is a primary reason
that many white club goers are happy that the club has
moved to its new location. Others argue that there can be
misunderstandings between them and the black deaf. Consequently, they do not feel comfortable with the blacks.

One source of misunderstandings is the sign language used
by the white and black deaf. Previous research (Woodward,
1976) suggests that while there are large similarities, white
and black deaf sign differently from one another. In the past,
schools for the deaf were often segregated, as were schools
for the hearing. Different signs developed in these different
settings. Consequently, misunderstandings between the two
groups may occur. Or, signs used by the black deaf may be
offensive to some of the white deaf. The deaconess of the
black deaf congregation, who was mentioned above, explained that

> while interpreting at a convention, she interpreted "prostitute" as
> "shameful lady" or "sell-body-woman" rather than fingerspelling it.
> That way the black deaf would understand. The white deaf under-
> stood too, but were offended.

While some white and black deaf are friendly with one another, perhaps knowing each other from school days when there were not separate schools, there is little association between the two groups. Due to geographical separation and to the feelings of uneasiness between the white and black deaf, one must necessarily speak of separate white and black deaf communities in the Chicago area. Thus, the findings of this chapter and the following ones should be limited to the white, deaf community where the bulk of my research was conducted.

The common bond of deafness only weakly unites the white and black deaf in Chicago. The prejudice of the larger society is also a potent force within the deaf world. Years of research indicate that the less educated one is, the more likely one is to be prejudiced (Simpson and Yinger, 1972). The deaf in America are less educated than the hearing. The median school grade attained by deaf adults as of 1972 was 11.1. For the United States population, it was 12.1 (Schein and Delk, 1974: 52). The actual educational attainment of the deaf is several years behind that of their hearing counterparts (Trybus and Karchmer, 1977). Therefore, if, as one counselor for the deaf contends, the deaf community is more prejudiced in favor of blacks than is the general hearing public, that greater prejudice is not likely to be due to deafness but to the deaf's being less educated than the general publice. However, no studies of this issue have been conducted, and I have found no indication of greater prejudice toward blacks among the deaf community than among members of the hearing world. I have found no indication of less prejudice either.

Sophistication and Education

Sophistication as indirectly indicated by education, though often education, in its own right, is another characteristic which structures relationships among members of the deaf community. As in hearing communities, deaf people generally intimately associate with other deaf people of their same intellectual sophistication and educational level. College-educated deaf are likely to associate with other college-educated deaf, high school-educated with high school-educated, and so on. Of course, friendships do cross educational boundaries. These distinctions of sophistication and education are used by deaf people in deciding what clubs they will attend. A deaf man who lives forty miles outside of Chicago is an active member in the north side club for the deaf in Chicago. Only rarely does he visit a deaf club in a neighboring town. He drives such a long distance partially because the Chicago club has more intelligent members—"better" people—than the club in the neighboring town. Therefore, socializing is more fun at the Chicago club. Whether one club's members are "really" more intelligent than another's is not the issue. That deaf people make such distinctions is.

Similarly, a deaf Chicagoan, a high school graduate, has been going to the north side club for the past two years, and enjoys it more than the south side club where he has been a member for years. He explained that a "better group" goes to the north side club. They were not all of the same "mentality" as went to the south side club.

The college-educated deaf use similar reasoning in explaining and justifying to one another and to me why they stay away from the north side club. From my observations, few college-educated deaf actively participate in the club, though they may pay dues. In the past year or two, though, some young, college-educated deaf have become active members, and one is now president. A young college graduate explained:

> We [his college-educated wife and he] sometimes go to the club, but not that often. Those who go to the club, for the most part, are on a different intellectual level than ourselves. It's OK to go and talk with them for fifteen minutes or so. That can be enjoyable. But not for hours at a time.

Another college-educated man, who lost his hearing as a teenager, explained in response to my question, "Do you

have any problems being accepted as part of the deaf community?": "In a funny way the only problem I have is with
the lesser educated deaf people." When I asked what he
meant by "lesser," he said:

> Lesser, not low verbal, not exactly right. The people from the
> state schools for the deaf. They grow up in schools. I have not
> shared their experiences. I have a little harder time relating to
> them socially. So really I don't. I'm not saying that all of them
> are the same way. No. But more or less the middle, the average
> deaf person from the state school. Not too keen on that. But for
> all the others, no problems.

Of course, many members of the deaf community, if not
most, are the "average deaf person[s] from the state school."
Or a key informant, a college-educated deaf man, though
not a college graduate, explained about going to a senior
citizens' club for the deaf where members were schoolmates
from earlier days:

> A person naturally likes to mix because of his own level. I go out
> of a sense of duty. I don't go there because I'm going to have a
> good time. I don't feel like I'm having a good time when I go
> there.

The well-educated deaf, especially those who are postlingually deaf and have acquired intelligible speech, are likely
to become leaders in the deaf community (Furth, 1973;
Jacobs, 1974). My own research suggests that these "leaders"
would be more appropriately characterized as people who
assume positions of influence in deaf organizations and often
serve as spokespeople for the deaf to the hearing world.
Although many are dedicated workers for the deaf, often
they are not leaders in the sense that deaf people follow them
and their ideas. Some may not even be well respected within
the deaf community, especially when they refrain from min-
gling with the "average" deaf members at clubs and social
affairs (Block, 1968; Sussman and Burke, 1968).
Because education and sophistication are used to differen-

tiate among members of the community, hard feelings may
arise. Those who are not college educated often complain
that some, though not all, college-educated deaf act like
snobs. They criticize such college-educated deaf by mockingly referring to themselves with a variation of the sign for
"college." By inverting the sign, literally turning it upside
down, it can be used sarcastically to criticize those who, in
the words of a deaf man, "think they are high." Translated
into English, the inverted sign of "college" means: "So you
think you are smart. Well, I am just uneducated, the opposite
of college educated." Further, the reasons given by the college-educated deaf for not attending the social clubs for the
deaf are often seen by the less educated deaf as excuses used
to hide the former's snobbishness.

A deaf woman explained her feelings toward a high-level
officer of a deaf organization in Chicago:

> I can tell you one experience I had. We [she and friends] went to
> an open house for the new . . . building [of a deaf organization].
> A guide showed us around the place. We were shown his [the
> officer's] office, and he and another man were in the office,
> sitting and talking. The other person was [also] an officer for the
> organization. They never got up to shake hands. Never came over
> to say, "How are you? Glad to see you." What kind of impression
> is that? When I see him, he never communicates with deaf people.
> He likes to go with the higher-ups.

When asked if she meant the higher-up deaf rather than the
hearing, she responded:

> Higher-up deaf people. Those people who feel big. I don't have
> much to do with him. I wish he would tone down and be more
> communicative with deaf, with us.

Many less educated deaf resent the behavior and attitudes
of college-educated members of the community who act as if
they were superior. Others may resent it, but they also
understand it. An active member in the state organization for
the deaf, the man mentioned before who regained much of

his hearing during World War II, explained his situation in the
following way:

> The out-of-town deaf people, the first thing they ask me is when
> did you graduate from Gallaudet [a college for the deaf in
> Washington, D.C.]. You know, we look about the same age and
> all that. I say, no, I never went to college. I never went to high
> school. Oh, whew! The status level changes real quick.

I asked if these were college-educated deaf, and he responded
that they were. When I went on to ask whether "they think
they're way up here and you're way down there" because he
didn't go to Gallaudet, he replied:

> I suddenly slip. They're still there [pointing to an imaginary
> level], but I suddenly slip.

As this same man noted, the feelings of superiority of college-educated deaf are not "unique in the deaf community.
You will find this in any community. This is what a lot of
deaf people don't realize."

While educational attainment and general sophistication
separate members of the deaf community, the communality
of deafness does draw together deaf people of different
educational levels—at clubs, organizations, and religious
groups. Friendships and marriages do cross differences in
educational attainment. I interviewed several couples where
one spouse was college educated and the other had not
graduated from high school. Yet, the shared experience of
being deaf does not completely neutralize educational differences among members of the community.

Age

Age is a third differentiating factor in the deaf community.[6] Unlike ethnic or racial outsiders, there are few deaf
children in the deaf community. Consequently, it is appropriate to speak of the adult deaf community. Less than 10%
of deaf people have deaf parents (Schein and Delk, 1974:

35). This is a consistent findings since 1910. This means, for most members of the community, that unless they attended residential school programs for the deaf as children, they were likely to be isolated in a hearing world rather than form part of a deaf group. The same holds true today, though deaf children may participate in such activities as religious worship where deaf adults are present.

The intriguing question becomes: How are deaf children and adolescents socialized into the adult deaf community? It is likely that such socialization occurs particularly in schools and to a lesser degree in colleges for the deaf, partially through deaf teachers. Clubs for the deaf may play a part for some teenagers. Deaf children of deaf parents are probably socialized into the community sooner and with less problems of adjustment than those who have hearing parents (Schlesinger and Meadow, 1972). Commitment to the deaf community is likely to be an outgrowth of involvement in deaf peer groups in childhood and adolescence. However, the above is only informed speculation. I did not explore that question, though certainly it is one toward which much research should be directed.

Apart from the fact that deaf children are not an integral part of the deaf community, age, as in the hearing community, structures relationships among the deaf. As I mentioned before, a senior citizens' club for the deaf has been operating in Chicago since the early seventies. It was established to serve the needs of the elderly deaf by providing an organization and place where they could meet, talk, reminisce, and keep in contact with one another.

At the north side club there continues to be antagonism between the younger adult members and those who are middle-aged or older. The antagonism centers on sponsoring athletic teams to compete against teams from other clubs for the deaf or hearing teams. The players on the teams are often the younger members of the club. Not too surprisingly, the middle-aged and older members are somewhat reluctant to use club funds to sponsor an activity in which they do not participate. A heated discussion about this matter was witnessed at the club one Saturday night.

Friendships are likely to be among deaf individuals of similar age. Again and again my respondents informed me that their friends were their own age and referred me to them. That is not surprising. In the deaf community, friends are often school or college classmates, or they may have initially been friends of friends or friends of their spouses. Attending the same educational program for the deaf for several years established a bond among deaf classmates and a wealth of shared experiences which are carried over into the adult deaf community.

While age does differentiate members of the deaf community, members of various ages do associate with one another. Young and old deaf participate together in formal organizations for the deaf—clubs, religious groups, and state and national associations. Members of the deaf community of different ages associate with one another at an open house of a deaf organization, the bar mitzvah of the son of a deaf couple, at a play put on by the local deaf drama club, or at a large birthday party for a deaf leader. Those deaf adults who have deaf parents often know many older deaf adults from their parents' era:

> As a child, a young deaf adult with deaf parents babysat for a deaf woman who knew her parents. Now that the younger woman is an adult, the two deaf women find that they enjoy one another's company. They talk about such things as astrology.

Again, the communality of experience and identification among members of the deaf community sets the scene for deaf people with diverse characteristics, in this case age, to come together.

COMMUNICATION PREFERENCE AND SKILL

The most important factor which members of the deaf community use in structuring relationships is communication preference and skill. Not only is this factor important in establishing relationships among the deaf, but it is crucial for understanding the deaf community's position in a hearing world. Put simply, there are two general modes of communication used among the deaf. One is called the oral method. The other is the manual method. The oral method in its "purest" form is based on speaking and lipreading. Manual communication is sign language and fingerspelling. Within the deaf community, there are oralists and manualists whom I will refer to as *speakers* and *signers*.

Speakers

Speakers rely primarily on speaking and lipreading when communicating with fellow speakers. When communicating with signers, they often accompany their speaking with signs, but they do not sign fluently. Those who are "pure" oralists in philosophy or communicative behavior are not part of the deaf community. A small number of these "pure" oralists are members of an oral association of the deaf; whereas others go it alone in the hearing world (Oral Deaf Adults Section Handbook, 1975).[7] Of course, the distinction between a "pure" oralist and a speaker is arbitrary. Speakers may accept as a member of the community an oralist whom signers reject as too orally oriented to be a fellow member. Speakers are likely to have had hearing parents and attended day schools and classes for the deaf where signing was not permitted.

Signers

Signers sign and fingerspell when communicating to their deaf friends. For many signers, their first language is sign language. They are native signers. Some have unintelligible speech and poor lipreading skills. Yet others speak and lipread well, even better than speakers. Signers prefer signing over speech or lipreading when communicating with one another. Rarely will they use their voice or even move their mouths with other signers. Those who do may be teased.

Signers reason that speaking and lipreading are for navigating in the hearing world, but they are not necessary among fellow signers.

Put very simply, sign language is a concept-based language of signs which has a different structure from English, but one which is not yet fully understood (Stokoe et al., 1976). Signs are composed of various movements of the hands in relationship to one another and to the body in which the hands themselves assume distinctive configurations. Within the last twenty years scholars have systematically studied the nature of sign language. Gradually it has been recognized that sign language is a complex language like English or French and not merely a set of gestures or "hand signals," as hearing people often refer to it. Sign language has a long but not yet clear history in America as well as elsewhere (Woodward, 1978).

Varieties of sign language exist. Many of those are the result of the mixing of sign language and English. American Sign Language is least influenced by English (Moores, 1972). The use of varieties of sign language displays the social organization of the deaf community. The more educated the deaf individual is, the more likely that individual will be familiar with varieties which approximate English. Varieties of sign language which approximate English are more likely to be used at formal occasions—for example, at a conference—than at informal ones. Social-educational, regional, and ethnic (particularly black-white) variations in signing exist much as they do in English (Woodward, 1976; Stokoe and Battison, 1975). Members of the deaf community can sometimes identify where other deaf individuals learned to sign much in the same way that accents identify where hearing people grew up.

Fingerspelling is just what the name implies: the indication of words by sequentially using different hand-finger shapes for each letter in the word. The hand shapes may pictorially approximate the letters which they represent. For example, the letter "d" is made by forming a closed circle with the thumb, middle finger, ring finger, and small finger, with the upraised index finger creating the stem of the "d." Proper nouns or words for which there are no corresponding signs may be fingerspelled. The better educated deaf are likely to fingerspell more often than the less educated deaf because the former are more concerned with making certain distinctions in their conversation that may not be possible to make with sign language. For example, "dictator" could be indicated in sign language with signs for "ruler" or "evil ruler," but the better educated deaf may choose to fingerspell the word. One may become fairly proficient at fingerspelling in a few weeks or months, but reading it well may take years.

Becoming a signer follows no single path. Those who have deaf parents who sign probably grew up as signers themselves. Others became signers in residential schools. Although signing often was not permitted in the classrooms of such schools, it was often allowed outside of the classrooms, in the dorms, and on the playgrounds. After leaving oral day school programs, many deaf individuals began to use signs which they learned from deaf adults. The hand rapping and monetary fines which were (and in some cases still are) administered to them when they were caught using their hands to communicate was not forgotten. The frustration and bitterness from failing to understand and to learn through the oral approach is still felt. Consequently, these converts are often the most adamantly opposed to oral education because they are the self-perceived victims of it.

Others, who did not immediately seek out signers, often found that their speech and lipreading skills did not gain them easy entrance into the hearing world. They were misunderstood and, in turn, misunderstood hearing people. A deaf woman, who is now a signer, explained that

> at the state school for the deaf, she went through the oral program. The school also had a separate manual program. Her teachers told her that she spoke well. When she left school, she spoke to hearing people, but they had a difficult time understanding her. Consequently, she stopped speaking to hearing people and instead writes her messages to them.

Similar experiences have influenced other deaf individuals also to become signers.

CLEAVAGE BETWEEN SIGNERS AND SPEAKERS

Signers and speakers are members of the same deaf community. They may attend the same religious organization, social club, or community gala. They also marry one another. In such marriages the speaker typically becomes a signer. Yet, through their feelings toward each other and their differential involvement with each other, strong divisions and at times antagonisms are created. That cleavage within the deaf community relates historically to the deaf's position within a hearing world. Particularly, it is an outgrowth of how educators of the deaf have traditionally felt it best to teach deaf children.

Historically, throughout the United States and to an even greater extent in other countries, the oral method of instruction has been dominant in schools and classes for the deaf. In 1880 that position was officially adopted in Milan by the International Congress on Education of the Deaf (Bender, 1970). At one time Massachusetts passed a law which disallowed the use of manual communication in the classroom (Mindel and Vernon, 1971). While sign language has been used for the education of the deaf in America since the first schools were established in the early 1800s, only recently has it become widely emphasized. Only since the early 1970s has the Chicago area begun to emphasize manual communication in the classroom. The combination of the two approaches, along with writing and any other effective means of communication, has been called "total communication" (O'Rourke, 1972). Total communication is now the predominent mode of communication in classes for the deaf (Jordan et al., 1979).

The oral philosophy was stressed in the hope and desire that deaf children trained in such a method would be able to move easily into the hearing world as adults. Perhaps more importantly it was also stressed due to the fear that if deaf children were allowed to sign and fingerspell with one another, especially in often isolated residential schools, then as adults they would marry one another and form deaf communities within, but apart from, the hearing world. Residential schools have historically been more likely than day schools to use manual communication in instructing the students or to permit the students to sign to one another outside of the classroom.

Alexander Graham Bell, whose wife was deaf and who was an influential supporter of the oral philosophy, voiced such fears in an 1883 paper, "Upon the Formation of a Deaf Variety of the Human Race." Bell (1883: 41) argued:

> Indeed, if we decided to create a deaf variety of the race, and were to attempt to devise methods which should compel deaf-mutes to marry deaf-mutes, we could not invent more complete or more efficient methods than those that actually exist and which have arisen from entirely different and far higher motives.

Bell criticized residential schools which isolated deaf children from the hearing world, teachers of the deaf who were themselves deaf, reunions of former pupils, organizations for the deaf, periodicals and newspapers put out by the deaf, and the "gesture language" of the deaf. All these and more were criticized because they constituted the

> elements necessary to compel deaf-mutes to select as their partners in life persons who are familiar with the gesture language. This practically limits their selection to deaf-mutes and to hearing persons related to deaf-mutes. They do select such partners in marriages, and a certain portion of their children inherit their physical defect. We are on the way therefore towards the formation of a deaf variety of the human race. Time alone is necessary to accomplish the result [Bell, 1883: 44].

This emphasis of hearing educators on oralism, and their suppression of signing among deaf children, has not gone unnoticed by the deaf. This emphasis is paralleled by the historical, though now changing, practice of white educators who emphasized standard English among black, Mexican-American, American Indian, and other-language minority children (Margolis, 1971; Heath, 1972). The educators seemed to reason that because outsider children will have to live at least partially in the larger social world, they need to be trained in its ways.[8] Good intentions motivated many of these educators. They went one step further, though. Native languages (whether signing, Spanish, black English, or another language) could not be permitted because they would hinder the acquisition of standard, white English, whether it be spoken or written. Consequently, just as deaf children caught signing in oral schools have been punished, so too have Mexican-American children been punished for speaking Spanish in Anglo-run schools. Educators from the dominant world were trying to mold outsider children into their image.

Through formal organizations as well as through friendships and informal relations, signers and speakers (or, as one informant characterized them, the "deafies" and the "rubber lips") organize the deaf community according to communication skill and preference. Informants told me that twenty years ago at a club for the deaf, the signers would congregate in one group and the speakers in another. Each made fun of the other. The signers mocked the mouth movements of the speakers, and the speakers mockingly imitated the signing of the signers. Presently, however, almost all who attend that club are manually oriented. An active member estimated that 70% to 80% were signers.

A new club, founded a few years ago in a northern suburb of Chicago, has become a haven for speakers. A few "hard of hearing" adults are involved in the club. Some signers do attend, though. They seem, however, to be co-workers or spouses of speakers.

A national fraternal organization for the deaf has several divisions in the Chicago area. One is attended by speakers, while the other two are primarily attended by signers. Though the oral division has a dwindling membership (active membership now numbers under thirty), its members·insist on being separate from the larger, manually oriented divisions.

The distinction between signers and speakers extends beyond formal organizations to friendships and informal associations. Respondents noted that most, if not all, of their friends had communication preferences similar to their own, be they manual or oral. Each group is not quite comfortable with the other's mode of communication. Speakers explain that sometimes it is difficult to follow fast signers, especially when the signers do not move their mouths. Signers complain that it is difficult to lipread the speakers or understand their modest signing.

A deaf woman, who prefers that other deaf people accompany their signs with speech and is an active member of the new north suburban deaf club, explained:

> Some deaf are sloppy in their signing, and I can't get what they're saying. I'm not comfortable with that set.

When asked whether she knew the Starers, a deaf couple, she replied:

> Husband, I understand. He's very expressive. She [the wife] signs too fast. After you get to know her. But she spells awfully fast. She's on my bowling league. And I talk to her, but she spells pretty fast. She can speak some.

Signers are equally uncomfortable with speakers. The wife mentioned above who signs too fast informed me that she is planning to quit that bowling league because its members are so orally oriented. Another deaf woman explained why she and her husband do not generally associate with speakers:

> If a deaf person doesn't sign, then you can get a headache trying to make out what they're saying.

A third deaf woman, a signer, explained that she finds

oral deaf people odd and funny. When you argue with them or discuss a point, their arguments seem strange.

She defined an oralist as

someone who had gone to an oral school, and though they might sign, they were not very skilled at it.

When asked if she knew B. R. and A. G., two deaf women, she answered:

Yes, I do. But I mainly see them at church. They go bowling, but other than that they keep to themselves. They are nice people, yes. But I enjoy associating with those who are manual.

The conflict between signing and speaking also disrupts family relationships. It is not unusual for deaf children who sign to communicate little with their parents who do not sign. As adults, their relationships with their parents may be bitter. Deaf siblings, too, can be divided by communication differences. For example, two deaf sisters in the Chicago area rarely see each other. Both grew up in the oral tradition, but the older sister married a speaker, while the younger one married a signer. The younger sister has retained her oral skills but has become more involved with signers. Rather than join the oral fraternal division at her sister's request, she remains in the larger, manual division where her friends are. The younger sister's husband claims that through lipreading he understands his sister-in-law and her husband, but they rarely visit one another.

While speakers and signers do marry one another, antagonism may exist in the early stages of becoming acquainted. A wife who was once a speaker explained about meeting her husband, who is a signer:

We met on a blind date at the CCD [Chicago Club for the Deaf]. When we first met it wasn't love at first sight. My husband is strictly manual. I was learning signs at the time, and while I was

good, I was not skilled. We had a difficult time communicating to
each other. I later asked my friend [deaf] why she had fixed me
up with that boy. A friend of my husband teased him about my
being oral. My husband's friend moved his lips in a mocking way.
A year or so went by and we got married.

While it is difficult to estimate the relative proportion of
speakers and signers within the deaf community, speakers are
a decided minority. Both the relative membership within the
oral and manual divisions of the national fraternal organization in Chicago and the proportion of the prevocationally,
adult deaf population who use signs (Schein, 1968; Schein
and Del, 1974) indicate that signers make up the bulk of the
deaf community, perhaps as much as 90% of the members.
Further, their numbers are likely to grow in the future as
total communication becomes more extensively employed in
educational programs for the deaf (Jordan et al., 1979).

Signing is not a sufficient condition, though it is a necessary condition, for membership in deaf communities. Those
who cannot sign are not members. Signing is an outgrowth of
becoming and being a member.[9] It is an indication of one's
identity as a deaf person and one's commitment to the deaf
world. It is perhaps the most obvious indication to hearing
people that one is deaf. Because deafness is a relatively
invisible impairment, deaf people would often go unnoticed
in everyday, impersonal activities if it were not for their
signing to one another. Also, signing often attracts stares,
unflattering imitations, and ridicule from the hearing. This
will be discussed in more detail in Chapter 5. Therefore,
"pure" oralists are viewed by members of deaf communities,
particularly by signers, as outsiders. Further, some signers
wonder if speakers are ashamed of being deaf. One signer
who attended a senior citizens' club for the deaf complained
that

> the president of the senior citizens club for the deaf was not
> proficient in signs, and therefore those who depended on signs
> wouldn't be able to understand him. Someone who could sign and
> talk should be president. That way all the members could under-

stand. Maybe the president was ashamed of being deaf and that's why he had not learned to sign well.

Signers may interpret speakers' not fully embracing signing as an indication that speakers are either trying to hide their deafness or are still hopelessly under the influence of misguided hearing educators. Either way, the speakers' commitment to the deaf world becomes questioned. That commitment is partially based on the conviction that hearing people have too long dominated deaf people's lives: in education, in jobs, even in the ways deaf people communicate with each other.

Similar types of antagonism are found among other groups of outsiders. For example, sansei, second generation Japanese Americans, may criticize their parents' generation, the nisei. The sansei criticize the nisei (American, born of Japanese-born immigrants) for trying to be Caucasian. The sansei criticize the nisei's desire for material possessions, their uncritical patriotism, and their covering up of the hostility and degradation associated with being interred during World War II (Kiefer, 1974: 75). Similarly, bisexuals and gays married to women are disliked within the male gay community because of their affiliation with the straight world. Their behavior shows a lack of commitment to the gay community (Warren, 1974). Members of communities of outsiders may criticize other outsiders who affiliate with or try to become part of the dominant world. That attempt may be seen as misguided. More importantly, it may be viewed as a repudiation of being an outsider and therefore a repudiation of those who find their identities as outsiders.

NATIONAL NETWORK

While the deaf community may be similar to an ethnic community in many respects (e.g., because of their strong identification with one another and many shared experiences), it is not geographically like a small, ethnic neighborhood within a large city. Through clubs, sports tournaments,

former classmates, co-workers, friends, deaf relatives, and the
TTY teletype system, deaf people scattered throughout a
metropolitan area keep in contact with one another. In fact,
through the above means as well as through state, regional,
and national organizations, meetings, and publications, deaf
people keep in contact with one another in ever widening
circles. A national network of contacts unites widely dispersed deaf people. These relationships begin at the local
level and build to the national level.

For example, clubs for the deaf and sports tournaments
which they sponsor help to maintain and create contacts
among deaf individuals. Members of one club for the deaf in
Chicago live forty miles from the city and others live twenty
or thirty miles away. No doubt the lack of activity in out-
lying suburbs and towns helps to draw deaf individuals to
organized activities in the city.

Sports tournaments, sponsored by the clubs and other deaf
organizations, draw deaf individuals throughout the Midwest
region. Deaf men and women come both to participate in the
contests, but perhaps more importantly to socialize with
other deaf people and renew old, but distant, friendships.
One deaf bowler explained:

> Hearing people can't understand why the deaf like to go to
> tournaments, bowling or whatever, and see other deaf. The deaf
> can figure and decide if they have enough money. The hearing
> can call over the phone if they want to contact friends. The deaf
> can't. At tournaments and competititions the deaf can get to-
> gether and have a good, sociable time.

From his bowling experiences, the deaf man knows deaf
people all over the country. Sports tournaments provide the
occasion for deaf individuals throughout a region and sometimes the country to come together, have an enjoyable several days, and in so doing reaffirm who they are. The same is
true for state, regional, or national meetings.

While most members of the deaf community cannot use
the telephone themselves, the invention and use of the TTY
enables deaf people to keep in contact with one another. The

TTY, short for teletype, was originally a combination of a telephone, a Western Union teletypewriter, and a coupler, which connects the two. TTYs have been utilized since the late 1960s (International Telephone Directory of the Deaf, 1974-1975: 7). Both parties must have a TTY. Rather than talking over the telephone, deaf individuals can type messages to one another. Deaf people with a TTY will be informed of incoming calls by houselights which are connected to the TTY and blink on and off. Newer models are available which are smaller than the Western Union teletypewriter. Some are portable and may produce an electronic readout rather than print messages on paper.

The TTY enables deaf individuals to "talk" with their friends who have one rather than drive to see them, write a letter, or depend on their children or neighbors to act as go-betweens over the telephone. Driving to see friends may lead to wasted hours if the friends are not home, or a surprise for the friends if they are home. Letters may work reasonably well unless last-minute changes must be made. Some children are too young to act as interpreters over the telephone. Others are reluctant. Some deaf parents do not want to depend on their children if at all possible.

Deaf adults are reluctant to depend on neighbors too. Often they will not ask neighbors to call for them until the neighbors have volunteered. Some will ask neighbors to make only business calls for them. However, even with the assistance of neighbors, the telephone call may not always be successful. As one deaf woman explained, the neighbor who does not fully understand the deaf person talks to a neighbor of another deaf individual who may not clearly relay the message to the second deaf person. The TTY helps overcome this problem. An answering service, available to those who belong to a local TTY club, makes it possible for deaf individuals to complete business calls successfully.

Consequently, two deaf sisters who live twenty-five miles apart now call each other weekly with the TTY. Before each bought one, they saw one another perhaps once a month. Friends who do not buy a TTY may be kept in touch with

less often than those who do. That is not surprising. Yet, in
the future, this development may create subgroups, however
loosely developed, of those who have TTYs and those who
do not. Perhaps status distinctions will be made between
those who own a TTY and those who do not.

The full potential of the TTY for keeping the deaf in
contact with one another has not yet been realized, however.
The TTY is fairly expensive compared to a telephone. Pur-
chase and installation may cost $200 or more for the cheaper
models, whereas the newer, smaller models and portables
may run close to $1000. Telephone bills with a TTY may be
high because it takes longer to type a conversation than to
speak it. The two sisters mentioned before run up thirty- and
forty-dollar monthly bills from talking to one another. Some
deaf individuals with poor written language skills are ashamed
to use the TTY. Consequently, in the Chicago area there are
only approximately 200 TTY's in operation, and not all are
owned by deaf individuals.[10]

While the TTY has helped deaf people keep in contact
with one another more easily, it has brought deaf people
problems that the hearing have faced for a long time: the
prank and obscene phone call and the wrong number. Deaf
individuals receive TTY calls where the callers will not identify themselves. Telephone voices are difficult to identify,
though distinctions can be made between friend and stranger.
However, it becomes almost impossible to identify the caller
of a TTY message. Obscene TTY calls have been received by
the deaf. Some deaf individuals complain that they receive
calls, but no one is at the other end when they answer. These
may be prank calls or simply wrong numbers. Deaf people
have fewer ways of knowing which kind of calls these are
than do the hearing. One deaf man suggested to another that
he unplug his TTY at night so that the flashing light which
accompanies incoming calls, presumably a wrong number at
that late hour, would not disturb him once he had gone to
bed. Even a bomb threat has been made to a college for the
deaf over a TTY. Modern conveniences bring modern problems.

Through these various means of communication and association, members of local deaf communities keep in touch with members of other local communities. Newsworthy events within the deaf community are likely to become common knowledge not only within that community, but also throughout the country. For example, while interviewing a deaf printer and his wife, the printer mentioned that

> he once worked in Washington, D.C., and wondered if Gallaudet College (for the deaf in that city) was still in a "bad" location. He recalled that just a few weeks ago a deaf woman had been robbed near the college. Both myself and his wife wondered how he knew. The husband explained that he thought he had been told about the incident at work from another printer whose wife was a cousin of the husband whose wife was mugged in Washington, D.C.

Knowledge of public happenings does spread throughout the deaf community. Consequently, some deaf individuals choose not to socialize much within the community. Gossip spreads too much, they feel. When at deaf gatherings, one cannot whisper in sign language. Consequently, if a conversation is to be private, it must be held away from the view of others.

> A deaf woman, whom I interviewed twice at length, drew me aside at a club for the deaf. Rather than sign to me within the main room, we moved to a hallway that lead to the restrooms. She needed to explain to me about her husband's drinking problem and did not want others to *oversee* her.

Because local deaf communities are connected with one another in a national deaf network, it is difficult for deaf people to escape their past. Knowledge of events which happened to them in one community are likely to follow them wherever they go. It may even precede them. Unlike those in a small rural community (to which the deaf community has been compared) where everyone knows one another, but who can escape by going to the "big city," deaf people often do not have that option available to them if

they want to remain among the deaf. As a counselor for the
deaf, who has deaf parents, remarked of a fight among some
deaf people in public:

> I could go away from . . . state [her home state] and start a new
> life and never meet anyone from my past life. But not with the
> deaf. This big mess [the fight] here. I don't care where Dick,
> Elaine, Pat, or Willy go. Eventually one day, wherever they land,
> the story will follow.

Exactly that happened. A deaf woman noted that

> several days later (after the fight) she received a letter from a friend
> in Florida who wanted to know more about the incident.

Even "wise" hearing people associated with the deaf community may not be able to leave their pasts completely
behind them. Since my parents are deaf, many people in the
Chicago area know them and consequently know of me. In
this case, though, the recognition has been a help and not a
hindrance.

Ironically, the interconnections among deaf people which
create what I have called a national deaf network are both a
blessing and a drawback. The national deaf network helps to
develop a sense of solidarity and shared identity among a
widely dispersed population. Yet it also lessens deaf people's
ability to control what other deaf individuals throughout the
country know about them.

CONCLUSION

Within the larger society, outsiders often create and maintain communities. Some of these communities are located
within well-defined geographical areas of the city: ethnic
neighborhoods, ghettos, or barrios. Members primarily associate with one another. For example, the social relationships
among the Italian Americans of the West End in Boston in
the 1950s was "almost entirely limited to other Italians,

because sociability is based on kinship, and because most friendships are made in childhood, and are thus influenced by residential propinquity" (Gans, 1962: 35).

Other communities of outsiders, though, may not be quite so geographically bound. Through marriages (both legal and symbolic), friendships, clubs, formal organizations, and a special argot or language, outsiders who are scattered throughout a metropolitan area *create* their community. The deaf community is such a creation. Through these various avenues of association, deaf people can keep in contact with one another in ever widening circles. First at the local level and gradually building to the national level, a network of relationships among deaf people is established. Through that network a sense of solidarity is created among a widely dispersed population.

Membership in deaf communities, however, is neither granted to nor sought by all who are deaf. Rather, it is achieved through identification with the deaf world, shared experiences of being hearing impaired, and involvement with other members. Most people who are audiologically deaf never become members. Some with lesser degrees of hearing impairment have been members for as long as they can remember.

Although the deaf community may appear to be homogeneous to the hearing, members of the community create distinctions among themselves. These distinctions are used in organizing relationships within the community. Some of these distinguishing characteristics are found within the hearing world as well. Race, sophistication as indirectly indicated by education (as well as education itself), and age are the most important of these. Due to the unique position of the deaf as outsiders in a hearing world, members of the community also distinguish among themselves based on communication preference. Signers and speakers find it easier to communicate with those whose communication preference is similar to their own. More importantly, speaking to fellow members is a vestige of the hearing world's domination of

and paternalism toward the deaf. Therefore, not fully embracing and using sign language may call into question one's
identification with and commitment to the deaf community.
Within deaf communities, members seldom face the difficulties and frustrations which arise when they navigate
through the hearing world. A sense of belonging and wholeness is achieved which is not found among the hearing.
Among fellow members there is no shame in being deaf, and
being deaf does not mean being odd or different. Within deaf
communities those who cannot "turn a deaf ear" now become the outsiders.

NOTES

1. See Padden and Markowicz (1975) for a similar conception of the deaf
community.
2. Most "coming out" among homosexuals, a process of defining oneself as
gay, seems to occur in interaction with other homosexuals. Gays too seem to feel
that being gay is a permanent condition (Dank, 1971, Warren 1974).
3. I met no one nor heard of any member of the community who lost their
hearing after the age of 20. Though such members surely exist, they are few. The
identity of those who lose their hearing after adolescence is already fully established as a hearing person. Entrance into the deaf world is usually not sought,
even when a successful adjustment to one's impairment is made.
4. Warren (1974: 154 161) argues that while secrecy and stigmatization lead
many homosexuals to the gay community identity as a gay person and membership in the gay community is fundamentally an existential choice.
5. Relatively few black deaf seem to join national organizations for the deaf
as well (Vernon and Estes 1975).
6. Age is particularly important within another outsider community, the gay
community. Middle-aged gay individuals may have a difficult time attracting a
sexual partner. Consequently, middle-aged gays may not frequent gay bars which
primarily serve a young clientele (Warren, 1974; Weinberg, 1970).
7. Approximately 220 deaf individuals 21 years or older are members of this
oral deaf adult organization Another 30 deaf individuals under the age of 21 are
provisional members (Oral Deaf Adults Section Handbook, 1975).
8. In a similar manner sighted professionals opposed for years the use of a
system of raised dots for reading and writing for the blind, and instead wanted the
blind to use raised, standard alphabet letters (Mindel and Vernon, 1971).
9. Some researchers have viewed deaf communities as language communities
where American Sign Language use is necessary for membership (Schlesinger and
Meadow, 1972; Padden and Markowicz, 1975; Markowicz and Woodward, 1978).
This approach is perhaps too restrictive, for it excludes speakers as well as many

signers who are not ASL users from being members of deaf communities. Yet speakers, nonnative signers, and native signers associate with each other, marry one another and recognize each other as part of the same community while also maintaining distinctions among one another.

10. Only 8% of households headed by a deaf individual reported having a TTY in 1972. Approximately 40% reported no phone at all (Schein and Delk, 1974: 71). Throughout the United States, deaf people are petitioning state public service commissions to lower telephone charges for those who use TTYs and to improve telephone services to such customers (e.g. operator assistance through TTYs). In many cases the deaf groups and their advocates have been successful.

3

IDENTITY

Outsiders confront everyday a world which is not of their own making. In both routine and dramatic ways they deal with and are reminded of their status as outsiders, perhaps through a disparaging remark, a job denied, or an ugly confrontation. For example, while there are no longer separate water fountains for whites and blacks, there still remain white-only country clubs. Hostility over busing is an obvious indication of the underlying tension between white and black people. Black children need only look around to see who are janitors and who are judges in order to realize that their skin color makes a difference. Many gays still do not disclose their sexual orientation for fear of being fired from their jobs or ridiculed by acquaintances (Ponse, 1977). Moral crusades against homosexuality make it clear that gays have a long way yet to go in their struggle for human dignity. The mass media further enhance the significance for outsiders of their status as outsiders. First, through the traditionally negative and stereotypical portrayal of outsiders (Bogdan and Biklen, 1977; Adam, 1978) and later, through a more empathic display of their struggle and lives (e.g., *Roots* or *Holocaust*), outsiders are reminded of the significance of who they are.

Outsiders whose families are outsiders are likely to be reminded by their families of their heritage. Through all these ways and more, outsiders realize that their status as outsiders is extremely important. Race, sexual orientation, physical disability, and so on become salient features of outsiders' *identities*—of who they are and how they feel about themselves.

It is not too surprising, then, that research indicates that black youth are far more likely than white youth to identify themselves in terms of race (Adam, 1978), or that Jewish children are more likely than Protestant or Catholic children to have extensive knowledge of their religious group (Yarrow, 1958). Those who monopolize reality have constructed the world so that it serves them. Therefore, they are likely to take for granted their favored position and the characteristics which support it. Outsiders, however, must regularly deal with their disadvantaged position. They are constantly reminded of how important are race, sexual orientation, physical disability, and so on. For example, Dennis Altman (1971) notes that society has made something portentous out of loving someone of the same sex and that therefore we should expect homosexuals to use this significance in establishing their identity. Thus, those characteristics which identify people as outsiders are likely to be of central importance in their identities.

The hearing world has made something very portentous of hearing and speaking, especially for those who cannot hear and speak. Therefore, among the deaf, the ability or inability to hear and speak is likely to be extremely salient. As children, the deaf were advised, encouraged, and even forced to develop their speech and lipreading skills because when they grew up they would have to make their way in a hearing world. And once grown up, they regularly confront the annoyances, frustrations, and setbacks of being deaf in that world. Therefore, in the same way that race is salient to blacks and sexual orientation is salient to gays, the ability-inability to hear and/or speak is salient to the deaf. However, while those specific characteristics are important to outsiders, the significance which they have for their identities may not be as straightforward as one might imagine.

Members of the outsider communities identify with their fellow members. As I noted in the previous chapter, among themselves a sense of belonging and wholeness is achieved which is lacking within the larger world. However, as I just explained, members of outsider communities also live within that larger world. Regularly they must deal with their status as outsiders—a status which is clearly disadvantaged in the larger world. Some outsiders, such as gays and those who acquired their disability in childhood or later, did not begin life as outsiders. They grew up to some degree as members of the larger world and from that perspective learned the crucial distinctions between being a member of the larger world and being an outsider in that world. Only later did they become outsiders, and one can expect that many then applied those crucial distinctions to themselves (Scott, 1969a). Many outsiders, again gays or the disabled, for example, have parents and family members who are part of the larger world. Such outsiders must deal with the desires of their parents for them to renounce or overcome their outsider status. Even those outsiders whose family and neighbors are fellow outsiders—for example, many black Americans as well as ethnic Americans—still confront the larger social world on a regular basis. Therefore, while race, sexual orientation, physical ability, and so on are likely to be extremely salient for outsiders, there is also likely to be a great deal of *ambivalence* about those characteristics (Goffman, 1963; Adam, 1978).

Members of outsider communities are likely both to *embrace* race, sexual orientation, physical disabilities, and the like as integral features of their identities, and to *degrade* themselves and fellow members because of those characteristics. Those traits are a basis for both self-enhancement and self-abasement. There is a tension between positively and negatively using those traits as part of one's identity. Though ambivalence will be personally felt more by some members than others, it should be seen as a *collective* experience. Ambivalence characterizes communities of outsiders who

82 OUTSIDERS IN A HEARING WORLD

must deal with a larger world. The opposing poles of self-enhancement and self-abasement are likely to change in their relative strengths. At various times one pole will be greater than the other. As I will note later, it is likely to take decades and even centuries for that ambivalence to fade. However, among many outsider groups, self-enhancement is beginning to dominate as self-abasement is rooted out.

Ambivalence among the deaf centers around the ability or inability to hear and/or speak. In becoming members of the deaf community, the deaf affirm and proclaim that they are deaf. However, it is difficult to forget the overwhelming emphasis of parents and teachers on being able to speak and lipread (i.e., being as much like the hearing as possible). Daily they are reminded that not being able to hear or speak is a drawback in a hearing world. Members of the deaf community are caught between their deaf community and a hearing world.

Beatrice Wright (1960: 130) observed that

> a person would not think of his hearing-impairment as a restriction if everyone else were similarly affected, just as we do not mind not being able to hear high frequencies.

Within the deaf community, members are more or less similarly impaired. Therefore, by itself, being able to speak or having some usable residual hearing does not matter much. Within the larger world, however, hearing and speaking do matter a great deal. Therefore, being able to speak and, to a lesser degree, having usable hearing takes on significance within the deaf community.

In developing a sense of who we are and how we feel about ourselves, we take into account the views of others. Sociologists and psychologists have coined such terms as "looking-glass self" (Cooley, 1902), "significant and generalized others" (Mead, 1934), and "reference group" (Hyman, 1942) in order to emphasize, among other things, just that point. Yet, not every other person's opinion will equally affect our self-identity and self-esteem. The judgement and standards of those whom we identify with, whom we feel we are like or want to be like, most affect our self-feelings. Members of the deaf community identify with fellow members. However, again they cannot easily forget the efforts of their parents and teachers to make them like the hearing, nor can they easily close their eyes to the difficulties of being deaf in a hearing world.

Ambivalence within the deaf community centers around several issues. It arises in terms of who is and who is not a member of the deaf community. Where should the boundary be drawn? It is a basic feature of how members view their impairment. Do they accept it or do they long to be hearing? Do they dwell on its drawbacks or do they take them for granted? Finally, ambivalence is involved in the conflicting emotions that members feel about speaking and signing.

COMMUNITY BOUNDARY

In the previous chapter, I explained that membership in the deaf community is achieved through identification with the deaf, shared experiences of being hearing-impaired, and active participation within the community. Ambivalence among the deaf gives rise to questions over who is and who is not "one of us." Where should the boundary of the community be drawn?

This concern is hinted at in the exclusion from the deaf community of hearing-impaired people who do not identify with the deaf. Members view such deaf people as misguided or as denying their true selves. More subtly, some deaf people with good speech, and in some cases quite a bit of usable, residual hearing, may not be fully accepted within the community. These deaf people are told by some members that they are "not deaf" (Schowe, 1979: 86). They are told that they are not deaf because in many cases they have not fully oriented their behavior toward the deaf. They are told that they are not deaf as a way of warning these deaf people with the skills of the hearing world not to "put on airs" (Schowe, 1979: 86). This second aspect will be discussed later. They are also told that they are not deaf because members may feel that such deaf people are not really one of them. Good speech and some usable hearing make them part of the hearing world, not of the deaf community.

The fundamental distinction between the deaf and the hearing is applied to courtesy members of the deaf community, as I noted in the previous chapter. This distinction is also partially applied by some members to would-be members who possess good speech and usable hearing. Hearing-impaired individuals who through their actions and attitudes would otherwise be part of a deaf community may be rejected by some members because they hear and speak too well. Such an individual is one hearing-impaired woman who speaks well and with amplification uses the telephone, went to a state school for the deaf since childhood and to a college for the deaf, and is married to a deaf man. She explained her situation in the following way:

> I find now it's the other way around. Because some of the deaf people feel that I'm hearing and I'm not totally accepted by them. And then again I'm not really accepted by hearing people. So I'm right in the middle. [The deaf] don't really accept me. They say, 'You're hearing.' [They say that] because they know I can hear and I can talk.

Yet such hearing-impaired people do receive a measure of acceptance from those members who tend to reject them. They are called upon by the deaf to act as mediators between deaf and the hearing worlds, as interpreters to the hearing. This clearly differentiates them from the hearing. As the deaf woman, mentioned above, continued:

> They [deaf people] can rely on me to do the talking for them [e.g., telephoning]. And in that sense they do accept me because I am somebody who can help them. Because they don't really want to turn around to a hearing person and ask them to do something.

The hearing and speech ability of this hearing-impaired woman creates a barrier between her and some members of the deaf community, but simultaneously allows her some acceptance by those who reject her. She is almost hearing, and therefore some members reject her. She is not quite hearing, though, and therefore members will rely on her for help in navigating through the hearing world. It is often only with the greatest reluctance that members of deaf communities rely on hearing people for such assistance.[1] As a deaf man emphasized:

> We don't need hearing people who can sign and are going to help the deaf. Like Tom [a hearing individual]. Those who say, "Hey, let me help you. I can interpret for you." They are on an ego trip. The deaf can do things for themselves, though such people act as if they can't.

Thus, members of the deaf community may be ambivalent about how to deal with a would-be member who speaks well and has a great deal of residual hearing.

ACCEPTANCE

Ambivalence occurs again when members view their hearing loss. Do members accept their deafness or do they mourn their loss? Do they dwell upon its drawbacks or do they matter-of-factly recognize both the limitations and positive features of being deaf? Some experience that ambivalence more than others, but collectively it exists.

Students of disability have emphasized the often extreme psychological adjustment that individuals who experience physical impairment must make (Barker et al., 1953; Safilios-Rothschild, 1970). The psychological reaction to physical impairment has been compared to a period of mourning or bereavement (Wright, 1960: 109). Ethnic and racial outsiders would not experience this mourning. They have been outsiders all their lives. The comparable situation, though, would be white people who wake up one morning and find themselves black.[2]

Members of the deaf community, depending on when they became hearing-impaired, may or may not have experienced

that mourning. No doubt some who became deaf in childhood and especially in adolescence reacted with grief. Others,
being born deaf or becoming deaf in infancy, were less likely
to suffer that specific adjustment problem. Like ethnic and
racial outsiders, they have been impaired all their lives. Many
have never known or would not remember what it is like to
be able to hear. Half of all prevocationally deaf people lost
their hearing prior to 3 years of age, and of course many of
those were born deaf (Schein and Delk, 1974: 16). A congenitally deaf man explained:

> I don't know what it is to be a hearing person. I was born that
> way [deaf]. I don't feel handicapped at all.

More important, members of the deaf community are
adults. No matter when they became deaf, they have been
impaired for years and decades now. It is unlikely that
mourning characterizes their adjustment, as it may the adjustment of those who recently became disabled. Whatever self-
pity existed from being teased, left behind, or left out by
family, friends, and neighbors, has faded in childhood, adolescence, or young adulthood, when deaf friends were made
in schools for the deaf and fulfilling relations were developed
within the deaf community. The bitterness may be remembered by all, but the despair is gone for most. A deaf man
who became deaf as a teenager explained:

> Who doesn't wish that he could have all of his hearing back
> [laughter]? No, that's water over the dam, a long long time ago.
> You must face reality. You don't have it. Why cry about it?

Few members of the deaf community grieve forever over
their loss (Schowe, 1979: 78). Some do, though. Several
hearing Jews have told me of deaf Jews who are skeptical
that there is a God; if there were, then why would they be
deaf? I have yet to meet such deaf people, though. Some
members may go to extra lengths in seeking to become
hearing. A deaf man who is actively involved in a Southern
California deaf community mentioned to me his plans to try

acupuncture. Other researchers have found deaf people who are disturbed over their impairment, although the research does not address whether or not these individuals are members of a deaf community.[3]

Having been deaf for years, members of the deaf community are likely to have a detailed view of both the limitations and positive features of being deaf. While some members may stress one more than the other, both exist.

DEAFNESS AS A NUISANCE

Deafness is a nuisance in a hearing world. A light-hearted column has appeared for years in *The Deaf American,* the "Hazards of Deafness," which makes just that point. In Chapter 6 I examine in detail how deafness and its accompanying limitations inhibit encounters between the deaf and the hearing. Here, I want to discuss how members of the deaf community view their impairment.

For specific and practical reasons, some members of the deaf community would like to be able to hear (or would not mind being able to hear). Members realize that deafness has its drawbacks. Beneath the realization that deafness has its drawbacks lies the recognition that it would certainly be easier if the world were somehow constructed a little differently, and an awareness of the fact that it will not be.

Several deaf men explained that if they could hear they could obtain a better job. They would have an opportunity to be promoted to foreman or, in one specific case, become a manager in a brother's business. But foremen and managers must use the telephone. Easy communication is assumed to be necessary for such jobs. Thus, with the realization that one's opportunities for advancement are blocked comes a realistic "desire" to hear. These men do not so much long to hear; rather, they recognize that if they could hear, then they might be able to hold jobs that are now denied them.

It is very understandable, then, that in a survey of 75 professionally employed deaf people, Alan Crammatte (1968) found that most, though not all, anticipated a higher level of satisfaction with their lives if they were hearing. These deaf professionals had accepted their deafness, but as Crammatte (1968: 133) notes, the anticipations of higher levels of satisfaction as a result of hearing were "realistic views of a moderately successful career and reasonably optimistic views of their potential had the handicap been removed." Equally revealing is that a few of Crammatte's respondents reacted to the question about their satisfaction if they could hear with, "I never thought of that." Their hearing losses were simply taken for granted. It is reality, in this instance the work situation, that shapes deaf people's view of the limitations which their impairment sometimes creates.

Better hearing would lead to easier communication with hearing people. A deaf woman who is divorced remarked that if she could hear it would be easier to communicate with her hearing "boyfriend" at work. A deaf woman of deaf parents sometimes wishes that her parents could hear so that they could have helped her develop better speech than she presently has. Better speech would help her navigate more smoothly in a hearing world.

Normal hearing would make it possible to enjoy more fully or benefit from some of the products of modern technology. Radios would become more than little black boxes. Television and movies would be more enjoyable if they could be heard as well as seen. A deaf man enjoyed seeing *The Sound of Music*, but wished that he could have heard it. Telephone conversations would not have to be completed through hearing go-betweens if the deaf could hear.

As noted in the previous chapter, one would not need to be dependent on hearing people if one could hear. Misunderstandings which result from the use of a go-between could be eliminated. A deaf man explained that

> sometimes when he has asked a hearing person to call for him and his wife, everything has not gone smoothly. The hearing person will talk for five minutes when all the deaf couple asked for was a doctor's appointment. After five minutes, the hearing person will say

"yes" concerning the appointment, but the deaf couple wonders what the entire conversation was about. At other times, the deaf man will have more to ask, perhaps wishing to be more specific on a point. However, the hearing person will have hung up and simply told him what the person on the other end said. It is too late for the deaf man to continue the conversation. Or the deaf man wants to be informed of everything that was said so that he can make the decision himself, and not rely on the hearing person who is calling for him. Yet, writing takes time, few hearing people sign, and spoken conversations between him and the hearing are slow. Being informed of bits and pieces of the conversation or told "yes" or "no" is not enough for the deaf man. Yet that is what happens.

Improved hearing would help those deaf who try to use the telephone to avoid embarrassing misunderstandings. A deaf woman fondly explained how several years ago

> she answered the phone and thought that a newspaper was calling in order to write a story about her husband, who was president of a deaf organization at the time. She didn't completely understand the conversation so she called her neighbor to come and talk for her on the phone. A newspaper representative was calling, but all the representative wanted to know was if she was interested in subscribing to the paper.

While deafness does not prevent deaf parents from raising healthy hearing children (or deaf children), several parents or would-be parents wished that they could hear their children's voices. A deaf wife, who with her deaf husband planned to start a family soon, felt that with hearing they could be more aware of what the children were doing in another room. A deaf mother believed that better hearing would make it unnecessary for her children to repeat so much to her. Another deaf woman recalled that two or three times she wished she could hear:

> When my children were young and they called mother, I couldn't hear them and wished that I could. At school plays my children might be singing. A person sitting next to me in the audience would tell me how well my children were singing. I wished that I could hear them.

A member of the deaf community mentioned the following
in explaining his wife's view of her teenage deafness:

> In the twenty-six years that we've been married, I have only
> heard her once say that she wished she could hear. That was the
> day my daughter was born.

In a hearing world deafness is often a drawback. Members
of deaf communities realize that. Therefore, for very specific
reasons and in particular situations, they would enjoy being
able to hear. It would help them in their daily activities. Yet,
most are not preoccupied with their hearing losses. It is taken
for granted and they know that it is unlikely to change.

BENEFITS OF DEAFNESS

While deafness is a drawback in a hearing world, at times
deaf people may not necessarily miss being able to hear.
Many choose not to use a hearing aid, even though they
would benefit from it.[4] Others use one at work when they
must interact with hearing people, but take their aid off
when they come home. Like ethnic Americans who could
improve their accents with training but do not bother because it is not that important to them, many deaf people
choose not to mechanically improve their hearing. Couples
gently chided and kidded one another in my presence for not
using or trying an aid or discarding it once it had been tried.
One woman never replaced her stolen aid. Years ago, another
woman tried an aid given as a gift by her uncle, but does not
use one now, nor does she intend to try one again. A deaf
man, who was not wearing his hearing aid when I interviewed
him, remarked:

> In fact I have a hearing aid. A lot of times I'm happy to take it
> off. I don't want to hear too much. Noise is too distracting and
> most of the noise that you hear is not necessary.

As the deaf man's remarks indicate, the putative flaw of
outsiders may have positive features which are not recognized

by the larger social world. Ethnic Americans can hold a private conversation in public by communicating in a foreign language. So too can the deaf. Ex-convicts may be able to use their inside knowledge in order to become security consultants for large corporations. A hearing loss provides some benefits which deaf people have come to enjoy. Disturbing and distracting noises are not heard and therefore do not bother many deaf people. One deaf man mentioned that the sound of an electric typewriter does not bother him. Trains, airplanes, and late-night, wrong-number phone calls will not wake many sleeping deaf people. Though children's voices would be welcomed sounds, their screams and yells literally fall on deaf ears. During several interviews with deaf adults, their children were talking so loudly or were playing the television or stereo so loudly that the noise was distracting and even painful to me. The deaf people whom I was interviewing, though, did not show any sign of discomfort. Most members of the deaf community appraise their impairment in a straightforward way. It is a nuisance in a hearing world, but the situation is unlikely to change. At the same time, there are some positive features of being deaf which are recognized, but are not manufactured merely to rationalize one's fate. As one deaf author noted, deafness can be endured by most members without self-pity but also without overlooking its very real limitations (Schowe, 1979).

BECOMING HEARING

As I noted in the previous chapter, some members of the deaf community do regain partial or even almost total hearing through surgery or fortuitous circumstances. Coming back from beyond the pale is not a totally pleasant experience, however. An adjustment to one's new condition must be made. New sounds are unfamiliar and distracting. Words are not immediately recognized, but must be learned and distinguished from the jumble of noises assaulting the ears. Once hearing has been partially restored, additional hearing may not be desired.[5] The man whom I discussed in the

previous chapter and who now has only a slight hearing
impairment explained how, as a young adult, he regained his
hearing, and his feelings about that restored ability:

> I got a job at the munitions plant, just down at the end of the
> street. At that time [early 1940s] they were making Napalm
> bombs. They sounded like a 150mm howitzer. The previous
> person had ruptured his ear drum. That's why they needed a new
> person [to test the bombs]. A terrific sharp blast. Had to keep
> your mouth open to equalize the pressure. Did it for seven
> months until the company lost [its] contract. We lived in [city],
> and we were one block from the railroad and I could hear the
> train steam whistle going by. I could hear them before, but I had
> to be up close. The city bus would go past the house shifting
> gears. I never heard that before. Sometimes hearing people
> [would be] talking on the street. It bothered me. I didn't have a
> good audiogram before and after to verify it. But my reaction was
> that I was hearing better. And I would sit at the table and Mom
> and Dad talking. All of this bothered me. It made me nervous. I
> had to get away from it. It wasn't a pleasant thing. A lot of
> people think you can hear again; boy it's wonderful. I didn't
> think of it that way. I had to learn to hear what these sounds
> were. Identify them.

"You were hearing a lot of noises, but you weren't really
picking out the words?" I asked him.

> Right! I had to learn to hear. Just like learning to walk all over
> again. These were weird sounds.

In a similar manner, the hearing-impaired woman mentioned earlier in this chapter who is on the boundary of the
deaf community because she does hear so well, explained
how she felt when her hearing improved after surgery:

> But at times I wish I could go back to where my hearing was 83
> db loss [a major impairment; it is now only a 20-30 db loss] in
> this ear because [laughter] when you have screaming children and
> you're in a noisy group and during that time [before the opera-
> tion] when the noise stopped me I could always turn my hearing

aid off and that helps the rest of you. But now I can't turn my
ear off. Once in a while I wish I could go back to [that time
before the operation]. Have my hearing improved more, no.

I asked, "How did you feel eight years ago when you had the
operation? Were you excited, happy?"

I was happy then. More thrilled about it. He [her deaf husband
with good speech] took advantage of it more or less [laughter].
Because like the first couple of nights when I came home from
the hospital, he said, "Oh, fine! I can talk to you when we are
laying in bed." When he started talking I jumped because "you're
yelling." But that time I was just getting used to hearing sound in
this ear, because I never heard sound. And so really [pause] I am
glad that I have the hearing that I have, but to have more, no.

Other members of the deaf community also realize that
regaining one's hearing has its drawbacks. It can be very
unsettling. Thus, members of the deaf community have
mixed feelings about their hearing loss. Their impairment is a
significant drawback in a hearing world. Yet, most realize
that it is unlikely to change. Therefore, as they strive to
establish their identities as deaf people in a hearing world,
they must deal with their ambivalence about being deaf.

COMMUNICATION

Members of the deaf community, especially those who are
signers, embrace sign language as part of their identity. Be-
sides being an effective means of communication, sign language is both a symbol of deafness and an integral part of
being deaf. However, sign language is not an effective means
for communicating with the hearing world. Further, as I
explained in the previous chapter, it has traditionally been
vehemently banned by hearing educators of the deaf. And as
I explain in Chapter 5, signing is stigmatized within the
hearing world.

Speaking, however, is highly valued within the hearing
world. It helps one navigate among the hearing. It is an extra

tool that some members of the deaf community possess. By itself, it is not particularly important within the deaf community. As I noted in the previous chapter, many signers with good speech do not even open their mouths when they sign to one another. Because of its significance within the hearing world, though, speaking takes on importance within the deaf community. Those who speak well can literally become spokespeople to the hearing world. Therefore, there is tension between signing and speaking within the deaf community. This tension or ambivalence transcends the distinction between signers and speakers, though certainly it is part of that distinction. It exists among signers themselves and is displayed in several ways within the community.

Speaking

Many deaf people cannot speak, or they speak unnaturally, without "normal" voice quality and inflection. This gives rise to several problems, as we shall see in Chapters 5 and 6. Such speech may be irritating not only to the hearing, but also to the deaf. Members of the deaf community may have sufficient residual hearing to hear speech, if not necessarily to understand it. A deaf *signer* who speaks well explained:

> We have a few diehards like those who were brainwashed into believing that they can speak good. There are two people at the ... club. I wish you could meet them, Jim Katz and his wife. His wife went to ... deaf school. Boy, she remains oral. You should hear her voice. I'm ashamed to be with her in public.

The signer's concern was for the harm which he felt oral programs did to the deaf. However, part of the sentiment which he expressed is similar to the hearing world's pity for and derision of those who cannot speak well.

However, because of the heavy emphasis on oralism, some deaf adults seem to have resisted learning spoken English. Some with good speech may refuse to use it with hearing individuals (Meadow, 1972). Others, though, refuse to use their speech because they think it sounds "funny."

Speech does make a difference within the hearing world. Deaf people realize that. Consequently, it is not too surprising that Allen Sussman (1973) found that the better deaf people rated their speaking (and lipreading) abilities, the slightly higher was their self-esteem. Further, members of the deaf community who can speak are more easily able (or are viewed by the hearing world as more able) to act as spokespeople to the hearing world. Therefore, within the deaf community, distinctions may be made between those who can speak and those who cannot, between those who have only a closed ear and those who have both a closed ear and mouth (Schowe, 1979: 70). Further, a "pecking order" among deaf leaders, according to speech and lipreading skills, seems to exist within some communities (Jacobs, 1974: 67-68). Those with greater oral skills may accord themselves greater prestige and esteem. However, other deaf people may not concur and may even tell those who can speak just that (Jacobs, 1974; Schowe, 1979).

This distinction and at times stratification within the deaf community, which is based on speech ability, is found in parallel forms within other outsider groups (Goffman, 1963). Historically, blacks in America have defined dark skin as undesirable and light skin as desirable (Ransford, 1970). Many blacks have gone to great effort to straighten their hair.

This ambivalence is also manifested in the changing patterns of leadership within outsider groups. Adam (1978: 61-62) speaks of a cycle of leadership within the civil rights movements of oppressed groups. The first movements seek the support of "liberal patrons" from the larger society. Second-generation leaders adopt to some degree the symbols of the dominant society. Only within the third stage of leadership does "militance among these groups bring leaders shorn of the symbols of conventional respectability." Thus, early presidents of the NAACP were white and some second-generation leaders had white wives. Among gays, the early Mattachine society sued for defamation when it was suggested that its members were gay, and second-generation leaders had wives and children.

A similar cycle of leadership has occurred within the deaf community. Early leaders were often sympathetic hearing educators or professionals, sometimes with deaf spouses or parents. Later, deaf people who lost their hearing in childhood or early adolescence and consequently had good speech became leaders. Now, however, comes the realization that previous leaders may have presented to the hearing a distorted view of what the deaf community is like. Therefore, there is a growing demand that deaf people without good speech be allowed to assume leadership positions, and they are (Jacobs, 1974; Jones, 1979).[6]

Signing

Speech has taken on significance within the deaf community because of its importance within the hearing world. At the same time, though, members embrace sign language as an integral part of their identity. However, because signing has been degraded for so long within the hearing world, some who are just becoming members as well as those who have hearing children may have some mixed feelings about sign language.

Deaf individuals who have not yet or are just beginning to find their place in the deaf community may be ambivalent about signing. A deaf woman, a speaker, who at an earlier time had not fully accepted her deafness and still evaluated herself by the standards of the hearing world explained her feelings about signing in public. As I discuss in Chapter 5, signing is an obvious indication to hearing people that one is deaf.

> Years ago, I didn't want to show sign language. Years ago, I would say ten, fifteen years now. At first I was the only deaf [person where she worked]. Then there were other deaf people, young, and they signed to me. And other people didn't think I was deaf [before that time]. I felt uncomfortable. But now it doesn't bother me anymore.

As the deaf woman became more involved in the deaf community, as her significant others became hearing-impaired people, signing in public no longer bothered her. Remember the deaf signer in the previous chapter who felt that speakers may be ashamed of signing.

The same shame may occur in children of outsider parents who themselves are not outsiders or are not as much outsiders as are their parents. That shame, in turn, shames the outsider parents who begin to doubt that they have nothing to be ashamed of. These children judge themselves and their parents and, in turn, are judged by other children by the standards of the larger society. The parents, though, do not quite measure up. Due to that shortcoming, children may be ashamed of both themselves and their parents. First- and second-generation ethnic Americans may be ashamed of the "old-world" ways of their foreign-born parents and grandparents. Hearing children may be ashamed of their deaf parents' impairment or of sign language, which is an indication of that impairment. Deaf parents know that. Therefore, it was with great pride that a deaf husband and wife explained that

> our 10-year-old son had to learn fingerspelling for cub scouts. He
> was thrilled because he already knew.

A deaf mother recalled, however, that

> our son was embarrassed about our being deaf. He never told his
> teacher that we were deaf. He didn't want to learn sign language.
> Until one time in school his class studied Indian signs. Our son
> wanted to be the first to know those signs. I explained to him
> that the signing of deaf people was similar to Indian signs.

Knowing that I had deaf parents, the deaf mother mentioned above and her deaf husband wondered if it was unnatural for their son to feel the way he did. It was not, because the son still clung to certain standards of the hearing world. Thus, hearing children's passing shame creates momentary uneasiness for the deaf parents about their own self-identity and self-worth.

Other members are more militant about sign language. They resent or actively oppose tampering with their sign language (McSweeney, 1975).[7] Attempts to change sign language, which seem to be primarily conducted by hearing educators, are not welcomed, just as the oral method is not welcomed. These attempts take various forms: the creation of new signs for which there were no previous signs, the replacement of previously used signs with newly created ones, and the emphasis of signing in standard English syntax rather than the use of American Sign Language (Nash, 1976).[8] All three attempts, which overlap to some degree, have grown out of the desire of educators, many of them hearing, to improve the English skills of deaf children. Controversy surrounding these attempts existed 100 years ago, but is particularly acute now (Fant, 1974). The third attempt is primarily debated by deaf and hearing educators and professionals (Bragg, 1973; Fant, 1974). The second attempt and, to a lesser degree, the first attempt attract the concern of the members of the deaf community.

Educators of the deaf, as well as members of the deaf community, recognize that deaf children and adults often have poorly developed English skills. Where the blame is placed, however, may differ. Hearing educators have traditionally blamed sign language for being an incomplete version of English and parents for not thoroughly pursuing an oral philosophy at home. Others blame the failure of parents and teachers to communicate effectively (i.e., to sign consistently) with deaf children from infancy. Research indicates that as practiced, total communication is more effective in developing deaf children's academic skills than is the oral method (Schlesinger and Meadow, 1972). However, there is a debate as to whether sign language should be modified and supplemented so that it conforms more closely to the structure of English.

Some deaf adults believe that new signs, such as those for forms of the verb "to be" (which are not a part of American

Sign Language), would help young deaf children improve their English skills. Others question how beneficial that would be. According to a deaf woman, an aide in a high school program for the deaf, it is not necessary for hearing educators to invent new signs for English words for which there are no equivalent signs.[9] Nor is it necessary for sign language to follow English structure. Members of the deaf community complain that too many separate groups are creating their own signs. Such groups operate at both the national and local levels. This will only lead to confusion, they argue.

Members of the deaf community may accept some new signs if they are seen as faithful to the pattern of American Sign Language. A deaf couple was satisfied with the signs for "try" or "attempt." "Try" is a long-used sign composed of the moment of both hands in a "t" position (hands clinched in a fist with the thumb sticking between index and middle finger) away from the chest, as if one were making an effort to do something. "Attempt" is similar to "try," except that an "a" hand (hands clinched in a fist with thumb adjoining the index finger) is used rather than a "t." However, signs accepted by one member might be deemed "stilted" by another. The signs for "to be" and its derivates fall into this category.

Many new signs, though, are seen as foolish, silly, or unfaithful to American Sign Language. A deaf couple felt that

a new sign for the word "carpet" was silly. The sign was the conjunction of two individual and long-used signs for "car" and for "pet." Together they were to indicate "carpet."

Such a sign for "carpet" shows a lack of understanding, insensitivity, or both for the sign language of the deaf community. A carpet or rug is not conceptually composed of a car and a pet. The creators of the sign must have been working from a phonetic sequence system, like English, where the sound of the word "carpet" was seen as roughly equivalent to the two sounds of "car" and "pet." These sounds, or morphemes, were then visually transformed into the signs "car" and "pet." Such creations do not respect the sign language of the deaf, though they certainly impose the hearing world upon the deaf. Hearing people who learned these sign systems would have difficulty communicating with many members of the deaf community. The couple who accepted the sign for "attempt" explained that some new signs which they had seen for "understand" were not acceptable to them:

> The signs did not conceptually follow ASL. The traditional sign is the flicking of the index finger from a closed hand position near one's forehead, as if the "light of understanding" had come to one. One new sign for "understand" was the combination of the sign for "under" and for "stand." The other new sign for "understand" was the sign for "stand" (the index and middle finger of one hand placed standing downward on the upturned palm of the other hand) inverted so that the palm is turned downward and the fingers of the other hand are underneath the palm, pointing upward and touching the palm.

As in the case of the sign for "carpet," "understand" is not conceptually composed of the concepts "under" and "stand," nor of "stand under," as implied by the second of the two new signs. In English the word "understand" can be divided morphologically into "under" and "stand." Transforming that division into the concept-based American Sign Language, however, becomes truly grotesque, as members of the deaf community realize.

Sign language is an important element of the identity of members of the deaf community. Therefore, tampering with sign language is strongly resisted.[10] Tampering with sign language is also tampering with the deaf community's identity. As one deaf adult said:

> You can cut off the fingers of deaf people and they will sign with their arms, and you can cut off their arms and they will sign with their shoulders [Furth, 1973: 34].

CONCLUSION

Members of the deaf community identify with fellow members. They give their allegiance to the deaf community. However, members have grown up and still live within a hearing world. They cannot easily forget the overwhelming importance that their hearing parents and teachers gave to speech and lipreading. Nor can they overlook the significance of speech and hearing in a hearing world. Therefore, like other members of outsider communities, they are likely to be ambivalent about who they are and how they feel about themselves. Collectively, they are torn between affirming and bemoaning their deafness, between looking to fellow members for self-identity and self-esteem and looking to the larger world which is all around them.

For decades and even centuries, members of the deaf community have been a dominated group. They have been repeatedly held up to the standards of the larger world and told that they have not measured up. Consequently, they, like black Americans, have traditionally had less self-esteem than members of the dominant world (Sussman, 1973; Simmons, 1978). Among outsiders, the self-belittling pole of that ambivalence has traditionally been stronger. But at least members have one another. I suspect that those deaf who are not members of the deaf community have an even greater difficulty in dealing with who they are. With no social support from the deaf, they go it alone in the hearing world. They live more marginal lives than do those who are members of the deaf community.[11]

The swing between the self-enhancing and self-deprecating poles of ambivalence seems to be changing among outsiders. Gays are coming out of the closet and demanding to be treated with human dignity (Humphreys, 1972). In the past two decades, a new black awareness has developed. "Black is beautiful" has become the slogan of blacks as they take pride in what before they often were made to feel ashamed of. The consequences of such self-enhancement movements are significant. Blacks are becoming less ambivalent about who they are. They are affirming their being black as they minimize the importance of the white world. This appears in the fact that the evaluation of skin color, at least for men, has changed within the black community. Light skin is no longer accorded higher status than is dark skin (Udry et al., 1971). It appears in the finding that black children no longer have less self-esteem than do white children (Simmons, 1978).

A similar awareness movement is taking place within the deaf community (Bowe and Sternberg, 1973; Woodward, 1973). Slogans like "deaf power" and "deaf pride" have appeared (Meadow, 1972). Both deaf and hearing educators are actively promoting sign language within classes for the deaf, though there is disagreement as to what kinds of signs should be used. Nevertheless, there has been a tremendous shift to total communication in educational programs for the deaf (Jordan et al., 1979). Research centers on deafness, leadership and training programs for the deaf, college-level sign language courses, and even degrees in sign language are being developed in rapidly increasing numbers. Sign language interpreters are out in the open now at meetings, in the court, in hospitals, and wherever members of the deaf community need their services. The deaf are among many of the physically disabled who have become politically active in demanding new legislation to insure their rights.

With this awareness movement among the deaf will probably come results similar to those that have developed within the black community: an increased self-esteem, less significance given to the trappings of the dominant world, and greater certainty among the outsiders as to who they are. However, such results may be slower in coming within the deaf community than within the black community. Unlike blacks, members of the deaf community must deal with families who are predominantly part of the larger world, in this case the hearing world. Also, unlike many other outsiders, being deaf is a drawback within the larger world, regardless of the attitudes of that world. Nevertheless, members of the deaf community are now actively asserting their identity as *deaf* people in a hearing world.

NOTES

1. This desire to be independent from and the skeptical attitude towards help offered by the hearing has been documented in the more general situation of disabled-nondisabled relationships (Ladieu et al., 1947).

2. A popular movie several years ago, *Watermelon Man,* was based on just that premise.

3. In a study of the deaf population in New York, Altshuler and Baroff (1963) characterized 62% of the respondents as stoically accepting their deafness; 8% as denying that deafness was a handicap; and 29% as disturbed by their deafness. The researchers do not indicate which of their respondents were members of the deaf community and which were not. Further, the term "stoic" suggests that the researchers may have been biased in assuming, as most hearing people do, that deafness cannot be matter-of-factly accepted.

4. Schlesinger and Meadow (1972: 3) argue that many deaf adults deprecate the value of hearing aids as well as speech and lipreading skills in reaction against the stigma placed upon their sign language. This does not seem to characterize the members of the deaf community with whom I talked.

5. The regaining of sight by the blind also seems to include unpleasant experiences and to be bewildering. Further, new laser devices to help the blind "see," have been criticized by some blind for providing too much information (Psathas, 1976). This is similar to deaf individuals who regain some of their hearing and then wish that they could turn off their ears as they once could turn off their hearing aids.

6. Part of this cycle of leadership among the deaf is due to advances in antibiotics since the 1930s. Many hearing people in their forties, thirties, and twenties would be postlingually deaf (i.e., they would have acquired a hearing impairment after the age of 3 or so) were it not for those medical advances. To the extent that medical advances have decreased the population of postlingually deaf people, there is less competition for leadership positions for nonspeaking deaf people (Pimentel, 1979).

7. Members of the deaf community may even oppose efforts to reveal certain aspects of their sign language to hearing people. Signing can be used as a boundary-maintaining device. Certain characteristics of American Sign Language use mark a person as deaf and are reserved for use with other core members of the deaf community. For example, some deaf community members were ambivalent about sharing sexual signs with the hearing. They felt that such signs should be reserved for intimate interaction among members of the community (Woodward, 1979).

8. A similar situation seems to be occurring in Great Britain, which has traditionally been more orally oriented than the United States. A deaf British social worker explained to me that a few schools for the deaf are starting to use sign language. However, instead of using British Sign Language, which is used by the deaf who sign, new sign systems are being developed to use in teaching deaf children because BSL is not seen as grammatical enough for educational purposes.

9. As technical terms increase in everyday language, educators of the deaf have felt a need to develop new signs for these terms. These signs would be used primarily in colleges and technical institutes where the deaf are educated. The graduates are then likely to carry these signs with them into the deaf community.

10. This opposition among members of the deaf community seems to be more than just a resistance to the "newfangled" signs of a younger generation, though for some it may be just that. The issues involved, however, are certainly more than what Croneberg (1976: 318) suggests:

> Oldtimers will maintain the superiority of the signs they used and are still using as compared with the newfangled signs used by the new generations. Educators of the deaf will maintain the superiority of the new signs they learned from one of several reputed masters of ASL.

11. Bisexuals are more likely than those who consider themselves gay to report guilt or shame about their homosexuality and to have lower self-esteem (Adam, 1978). Gays have greater social support from the gay community than do bisexuals (Warren, 1974).

4

DEVIANCE
AMONG THE DEAF

All groups develop ideas of what is acceptable behavior and what is unacceptable behavior. Groups praise some behavior but condemn others. Groups may establish rules and laws in order to formally enact those ideas. Or those ideas may remain as common understandings among the members of a group without being transformed into rules or regulations. In either case, members of the group become upset when someone acts in a way defined as unacceptable. The unacceptable behavior is deviant. In this chapter, deviance is "behavior that some people in a society find offensive and which excites--or would excite if it were discovered in these people disapproval, punishment, condemnation, or hostility" (Goode, 1978: 24-25). Members of a group do not have to use the term "deviant" for behavior to be deviant from a sociological perspective. Whatever terms members of a group call a particular behavior, the important point is that members are offended by it.

Those who create and control the larger social world define what is deviant. What is deviant to one segment of society, though, may not be deviant to another segment. Often outsiders are defined by members of the larger social

world as deviant. The behavior and characteristics of outsiders are disapproved of or condemned by the larger social
world.

Outsiders, though, also decide what is deviant within their
communities. Many times what is deviant within a community of outsiders is also deviant within the larger social world.
Remember, I noted in Chapter 2 that outsiders are partially
socialized within the larger social world. Therefore, characteristics which are used to distinguish among people within
the larger social world are often used by outsiders to distinguish among themselves. The same holds true for deviance. It
is not surprising then that robbery is deviant within both the
gay and straight worlds. However, there may be differences as
well. In Chapter 2, I explained that some characteristics
which outsiders use to differentiate one another relate to
their position as outsiders in the larger social world. The same
holds true for some behaviors which outsiders consider deviant.

In order to understand what is considered deviant within a
group of outsiders, we often must uncover the members'
perceptions of how they stand vis-à-vis the larger society. An
outsider community's system of meanings partially derives
from the community's perception of its relationship to the
wider society. Acts which call into question that system of
meanings are considered deviant because they jeopardize the
outsider community's perceived or desired relationship with
the wider society. For example, in nudist camps there are
rules for how members are to conduct themselves (e.g., no
alcoholic beverages, no staring). These rules are relatively
strict compared to some of the standards of interpersonal
behavior in clothed society. These rules are used in part by
nudists as a way of upholding among themselves an image of
respectability which the dominant clothed society does not
grant them (Weinberg, 1965). Therefore, to understand why
certain behaviors are deviant within the deaf community, one
must examine their relationship to the larger, hearing world.

In this chapter I examine one deviant act within the deaf
community: peddling among the deaf. As I explained in the

previous chapters, members of the deaf community identify with and are committed to their fellow members. While there is ambivalence among members, their significant others, those whose opinions and judgements are important to them, are deaf. In the work world, which is controlled by the hearing, the situation changes somewhat. What Heiss and Owens (1972: 363) note in the following passage about black Americans could be applied to the deaf too.

> At the same time, the evaluation of some traits may be importantly affected by persons outside the black community. These are traits which are subject to frequent evaluation by whites, and those less subject to the development of subcultural norms. They are those in instrumental areas in which whites have important control over the black man's fate and can therefore impose his norms. Thus, for those traits that operate in the worlds of school and work the opinions of whites are going to weigh heavily for most blacks.

In the following pages I explore peddling by the deaf and how it is related to the identity of the deaf community in the hearing world. The nature of peddling is described. The reaction of the deaf community to peddling is presented, and the reasons for that reaction are analyzed. The reaction of the community to peddling and the reasons given for those reactions help us understand how the deaf see themselves in a hearing world. By analyzing the deviant status of peddling within the deaf community, we better understand the identity of outsiders in a hearing world.

PEDDLING

Peddling by the deaf is a form of selling. Manual alphabet and sign language cards, which have a few basic signs printed on them, or small items such as pens, needles, or key chains are peddled. In that peddling is selling, it is different from begging.

Peddlers may work alone, in pairs, or for a boss who manages a group operation. According to a peddler who has written a small pamphlet about peddling, almost all deaf peddlers work alone or in pairs. Those who work in pairs are often husband-wife teams (Long, 1978). Large group operations may be few. According to the peddler-turned-author, less than ten groups of five or more peddlers probably exist in the United States. At least one or two group operations may be quite large, though.

One individual, now in his seventies and known as the King of the Peddlers, has headquarters on the East Coast and in the Midwest, and for a short time had an office on the West Coast. He has been selling, as he calls it, for more than fifty years. In the past, as many as 100 people worked for him, and he printed and manufactured the items that he sold. Now his staff has dwindled to 20—12 in the East and 8 in the Midwest -and he buys his stock. Over the years, hundreds of people have peddled for him. Deaf critics charge that he lured uneducated students from southern schools for the deaf to peddle for him. He claims, though, that he never went inside a school for the deaf in order to recruit workers.

The King of the Peddlers provides the stock and the cars for transportation. Therefore, his employees split their earnings fifty-fifty with him. The peddling author also claims that most pairs which are not husband and wife teams also operate on a fifty-fifty basis. Drivers, who manage the operation and own the cars, take half of the money of the deaf people who peddle under them (Long, 1978). However, a peddler who worked briefly for the King of the Peddlers claims that the employees receive very little of the profits, as little as 25%.

The King of the Peddlers' operation was once so successful that he owned a block of buildings in Chicago. However, the Internal Revenue Service investigated him in the late 1940s and early 1950s, and ordered him to pay some $60,000 in delinquent taxes. Consequently, he sold many of his holdings. He claims that he was not aware of any requirement to pay taxes. Most group operations, though, are not as large nor as successful as the King of the Peddlers'.

The King of the Peddlers sees himself as a businessman who runs a respectable operation. He opposes selling sign language or fingerspelling cards (also known as ABC cards) because they are worth little and can be sold for large profits, and because the activity is similar to begging which plays on people's sympathy for the deaf. Therefore, he claims to sell only "useful" items—pens, needles, and the like. The peddler-turned-author makes a similar claim about running a respectable business, though he has no qualms about selling ABC cards:

> Deaf peddlers are not soliciting charity. Deaf peddlers are independent businesspersons who are in business for a profit to earn a living (Long, 1978: 6).

Peddling takes place in taverns, restaurants, stores, libraries, public transportation, or wherever people congregate. The King of the Peddlers claims not to sell door-to-door because crowds are better. However, deaf individuals and their hearing neighbors have been approached at their homes by deaf peddlers.

Peddlers may live in one location and work in surrounding areas, as one informant and his wife do, or they may travel from city to city. In a group or pair operation, peddlers may drive into town and all but the driver fan out and cover the major streets and establishments. The driver meets the peddlers on the other side of town or picks them up at a prearranged location (Myers, 1964; Long, 1978).

The informant mentioned above who briefly worked for the King of the Peddlers discussed the places he found attractive for peddling. Fairs are an excellent place for peddling. Many farmers and rural people attend who have never before seen peddlers. Consequently, they are willing to buy from the peddlers. Airports are also lucrative places of business, due to the large turnover of people. Sunday nights, when travelers are returning from a visit, were deemed by my informant especially good times to peddle. Peddling at the

Chicago O'Hare Airport is illegal, though the law is often not enforced. Factories, especially at lunchtime, when two or three shifts of workers can be approached as they leave the plant to eat, are also desirable places for peddling. Downtown Chicago, however, is a bad place for business. According to my informant, the people are in a sour mood and always in a hurry.

This same peddling informant explained what were the best times of the day or of the year to peddle. Three in the afternoon to seven at night was the best time for peddling at shopping malls. Crowds were greatest then. Further, before Christmas was a good time for peddling, but after it was not. People had little money then. Business picked up again around Valentine's Day. Summer was a good season for peddling, due to the warm weather and the many fairs that took place.

The general strategy of the peddler is to approach an individual and hand that person a card with a printed or hand-written message which might read:

> SMILE
> DEAF
> EDUCATIONAL
> SYSTEM
> Please pardon my intrusion,
> but I am a DEAF-MUTE trying
> to earn a decent living.
> Would you help me by buying
> one of these cards?
> Pay whatever you wish . . .
> THANK YOU AND MAY
> GOD BLESS YOU ALL.
> THANK YOU!
> Hand alphabet used by the Deaf
> throughout the world. Easy to learn.
> [found at O'Hare Airport]

These cards, and there are over 100 different kinds of them (Long, 1978), are distributed to as many people as will take them or they are placed next to people who are sitting. The cards are collected if they or the small items which are advertised are not bought.

The above-mentioned informant has learned through experience that giving the card to a potential customer yields a lower rejection rate than merely putting it near them so that they may read it. The latter approach makes it very easy for the potential customers to ignore or reject the "sales pitch." Further, the peddler explained that when he approaches a group of individuals, if one individual gives money, then others follow in buying the small item he offers. An imitation or modeling effect seems to take place.

The informant and his wife both feel that the refusal rate is higher now than before. The peddler attributed that to the rising cost of goods. He estimated that the refusal rate approached 80%. The peddling author estimates that the refusal rate is between 20% to 70% (Long, 1978). On a successful day, the informant and his wife might earn $70, though in the past it may have been $100. However, peddling is not an everyday activity. It is tiring work. Locations must be changed often. Now and again police do hassle peddlers. Bad climate may curtail activities. Therefore, while peddling can be lucrative for some--for example, the King of the Peddlers--it does not seem to be for most. The peddling couple who served as informants lived in an undistinguished apartment with little furniture and few fixings. The peddling author tells a similar story. He estimates that the typical yearly earnings for most peddlers are between $2000 and $5000 (Long, 1978).

Deaf men and women peddle as well as children. College-educated deaf and the less educated deaf peddle. Some observers feel that the latter are more likely to be drawn into that occupation and then exploited by bosses (Myers, 1964). Some hearing people pose as deaf peddlers. Generally, that impersonation is illegal. The peddling author contends that such impersonators are not only deceiving the public, but they are also taking money which rightfully belongs to the deaf community (Long, 1978).

As in the case of blind beggars (Scott, 1969a), deaf peddlers are often not destitute or unqualified for work. Some
peddlers are well educated. Others, who may not have much
formal education, have developed a keen sense of what strategies will and will not work when peddling.[1] The deaf
informant mentioned above is one example. Another deaf
man, an ex-peddler, portrayed himself as a deaf-mute when
peddling. Although his speech was reasonably intelligible, he
felt this strategy increased his chances of success. Peddling is
not a last resort for many who peddle. For some who are
poorly educated and unsophisticated it may have seemed an
attractive opportunity. These are the deaf, according to some
observers, who are most likely to be exploited.

THE DEVIANCE OF DEAF PEDDLING

Historically, the deaf have been opposed to peddling by
the deaf. As early as the 1800s, complaints were made that,
while stringent laws had been enacted in several states for the
repression of tramps and beggars, an exception was being
made for the deaf and other unfortunate classes of humanity
(Fay, 1879). Such legislation was felt to be an insult to a
respectable segment of the community who neither needed
nor desired such favors.

In 1910 and then in revised form in 1934, the National
Association of the Deaf adopted the following resolution:

Whereas, There have been numerous instances of peddling by
irresponsible deaf persons, wherein the purpose was not to give
honest value for the money received but to mulct the public by
offering valueless articles and relying upon the pity of the buyer
for the deafness of the salesman, thus using deafness as a pretext
for securing money, be it

Resolved, That the Association places its most vigorous condemnation upon this practice and upon all who engage in it, and
call upon the self-respecting deaf everywhere to protect their
good name by relentlessly extirpating this form of begging [Best,
1943: 277].

In the late 1940s, the National Fraternal Society of the Deaf (NFSD) campaigned to end the practice of peddling by the deaf. Monthly articles appeared in *The Frat,* the official publication of the NFSD, criticizing peddling and quoting articles from newspapers when peddlers were apprehended by the police, fined, and asked to leave town. An excerpt from a letter from a Pacific Coast division of the NFSD was posted on the bulletin board of a club for the deaf in Chicago in an effort to oust from membership in the club the King of the Peddlers, who was named as a leader of a peddling gang. The King of the Peddlers filed suit. Several years later, and after the suit was dropped, a commission was established to regulate peddling. The commission never proceeded beyond formality because of the prohibitive expense involved and the consensus that administration of the code to regulate peddling would be difficult (The Frat, 1953; Sullivan, 1976). That same club for the deaf in Chicago has now changed its ruled to permit peddlers to become members as long as they are of "good character" and behave appropriately.

While peddling is often legal, most members of the deaf community are opposed to it. Although there is not unanimity of opinion within the community, the feelings range from disgust to a lack of concern. Active support for peddling is absent. One deaf man remarked:

> I have no use for them [peddlers]. To me, they are a parasite on the deaf community. They are an insult. I personally resent them.

Another, equally opposed to peddling, expressed his feelings in a different manner:

> I can summarize that [feelings toward deaf peddlers]: When one walks into the office, they always call me to throw them out and I'm happy to do so.

Some deaf people, though, perceive a complexity in the situation of deaf peddlers. A deaf vocational counselor explained:

Now take it from me, I'm in the field of vocational rehabilitation.
Some of the kids they [a deaf peddling organization] recruit are
multiply handicapped [by which he meant low intelligence and
not physical handicaps]. To be perfectly honest with you, I'd
have a hell of a time placing them. So this [peddling] is getting
[them] off the street. Now this doesn't mean I accept it, but
there is a place for everybody. . . . So, it's a black mark on the
deaf. What they do is small. Government, so much graft. You see
a lawyer, the fees are exorbitant. The whole society is out of
whack. So what the deaf do. Listen, I don't accept it really.

Another man remarked that jobs found by vocational rehabilitation services for deaf peddlers were often poorly paid.

Some deaf people, rarely the well-educated deaf, do not
feel it is their business how deaf peddlers earn their money.
One deaf person remarked that peddling did not bother him:
It was the peddlers' business. He just let them alone. Another
noted, somewhat dramatically, that it was a free country.
The Nazis did not control it. Therefore peddlers could do
what they wanted. The peddling author claims that deaf
peddlers are well liked and are respected by other deaf people
(Long, 1978). No doubt, some peddlers are liked by some
members of the deaf community.

Typically, though, the deaf not only hold unfavorable
opinions about peddling but actively oppose it through their
behavior. Many deaf people are approached by peddlers who
are not aware of the person's deafness. The peddling author
claims that "when a peddler meets another deaf person on
the street, both greet each other joyfully and engage in a
friendly chat" (Long, 1978: 20). Not so, according to my
deaf respondents. The deaf refuse to buy from peddlers,
question their behavior, or demand that they leave the neighborhood. Some, who are embarrassed about peddling or
apprehensive about what a peddler might do to them, do not
indicate that they are deaf when they refuse to buy. Others
ask their neighbors or fellow workers not to buy. Some
advise young deaf people about peddling. Deaf people may
refuse to associate with peddlers informally or at clubs for
the deaf. Others, though, associate with peddlers because

they are enjoyable and have many interesting experiences from their travels, but disapprove of and question peddlers' behavior. Some deaf simply do not discuss the subject with peddlers. Although the majority of the deaf community oppose peddling through individual encounters with peddlers, some oppose peddling in more formal ways.

A deaf man, while waiting at an airport, was approached by four deaf peddlers. He complained to a policeman, who did nothing. The man then wrote a letter of protest to the state association of the deaf where the airport was located, and the letter was ultimately forwarded to city officials. The officials replied that in the future peddlers would be dealt with more strictly at the airport.

Those who do oppose peddling in more formal ways—for example, the man approached by four peddlers at the airport or those who managed the antipeddling campaign for the NFSD—might be considered spokespeople for the deaf. Certainly they are better educated than the typical deaf person. They also have greater abilities than do most deaf people to use more formal means of opposition to peddling.

Throughout the deaf community, whether through individual acts of face-to-face refusal and confrontation or through formal opposition of letters and campaigns, most of the deaf are opposed to peddling. Not one deaf person I talked with, except those who actively peddled, supported peddling. No deaf person, including those who felt peddling was none of their business, mentioned having ever bought anything from a deaf peddler. Opposition to peddling is not confined to any segment of the deaf community. Young and old, men and women, the college-educated and the grammar school-educated are opposed to it. Peddling, though, is probably more vehemently opposed by the well-educated, professional deaf than those less educated. This probably reflects the former's greater interaction with a hearing world, and therefore a greater concern with the impression that peddling creates for the hearing. I will explore this later.

Yet, why should peddling be considered deviant within the deaf community when in many localities it is legal? Deaf people provide several reasons for their opposition to peddling. The one voiced most often and which seems most important is that peddling spoils their reputation among the hearing. As one woman explained:

> They [deaf peddlers] give deaf people a bad name, and they are trying to get other hearing people to feel sorry for them and it doesn't help [the deaf].

Peddlers are seen by the deaf as presenting a false image to hearing people of the deaf as incapable or unwilling to work. One deaf person commented that due to peddlers, the deaf must try even harder to prove that they are good citizens. The deaf perceive themselves as capable people, but peddlers present an image contrary to these self-perceptions.

The deaf also fear hearing people may think that all deaf people are peddlers. As one woman explained:

> If you've never met a deaf person, never seen one, and the first [encounter] is with a peddler, naturally they [hearing people] will assume that all deaf are the same.

Deafness is an invisible impairment, and, as one deaf man remarked, "You can see blind people by their canes, but normally [unless deaf people are signing to one another] you don't notice deaf people." A peddler may be the first deaf person or the most obvious instance of a deaf person that hearing people meet.[2]

Hearing people may or may not believe that all deaf people are peddlers. Yet, some deaf people have experienced situations where hearing people either asked or assumed that they were peddlers. One couple recalled that

> while lost on the north side of town, they went into a tavern to ask for directions. The husband wrote to the bartender for directions. Assuming that he was a peddler, the bartender began to give money

to the deaf man. The deaf man indicated that money was not what he wanted. Nevertheless, he was embarrassed.

In another situation, a vocational counselor for the deaf remarked of an executive:

> He couldn't understand what I meant by deaf people. He said, "You mean those people out at the airport who use hand signals." Like they couldn't do anything else but peddle.

While occasions of mistaken identity may be isolated, they serve to reinforce the deaf's opposition to peddling.

Some deaf people are particularly opposed to peddling at airports. They note that thousands of people, from both the United States and foreign countries, come through the airport daily. One or two peddlers can present a bad image of the deaf to a large number of hearing people. As I have already explained, though, for the same reason that the deaf are opposed to peddling at an airport, it is a lucrative place for business.

The deaf feel that their loss of hearing is their only disability. One deaf woman remarked:

> I think they [peddlers] should work. . . . I think it's too bad, but they should get out and work. . . . The only thing wrong with the deaf is that they can't hear, that's all that's wrong with them. They have good legs, good eyes, good bodies. They should get out and work. They don't have to go begging on the street.

Several deaf people mentioned that if peddlers were crippled or disfigured, then their peddling would be understandable. Yet deaf peddlers are typically capable of work.[3]

What is meant by work, though, differs between peddlers and the remainder of the deaf community. As I noted before, the several peddlers that I interviewed remarked that peddling is hard work and they sold "useful" items. Yet, many of the deaf view peddling as begging because it is not equivalent to the "honest" work they do. One man noted that he would rather be unemployed, and he was for a time, than peddle. Another deaf man remarked that he would not object quite so much if peddlers sold items that he would want himself, but cards and cheap pens were simply not desired. A deaf woman felt that it was more appropriate to accept welfare, which she had for a short time, than to peddle, because welfare came from the taxes that you paid. The deaf view peddling as dishonest work because it plays on the misguided sympathy of hearing people.[4]

The deaf also complain that peddlers can work only a few hours and make a great deal of money. One woman mentioned that in a day peddlers could make $200 or $300, whereas she would not make that much in a week. A retired printer noted that a stack of 1000 ABC cards might cost only $5.00 to print, and each would be sold for $.25 (which was confirmed by a peddler). The peddling author also claims that between $.25 and $1.00 is typically paid for a card, with the average being $.35 (Long, 1978). Peddling is an easy way of pocketing $20 or $30 in an hour or two of "work," concluded the retired printer. As one man put it:

> Some of them [peddlers] make more money than I do and that's what I resent the most. They don't pay taxes; have responsibilities like other deaf people. . . . A lot of people I work with [in] sign language classes [which he teaches], they say, "Oh, I saw this woman coming in, selling those things. I bought one." I say don't ever do it again. . . . Yeh, I say there's nothing poor about them. They make more money than you.

Others note that some peddlers live in fancy homes and buy expensive clothes. It is unlikely, though, that most peddlers do so well, even if popular sentiment among some of the deaf portrays peddlers as well off (Myers, 1964).[5] The few successful peddlers seem to be the most visible ones.

Those deaf people who are not actively opposed to peddling would not themselves peddle. They claim that they lack the ability or personality to continually and aggressively confront people. Others find it embarrassing. One deaf man recalled that while traveling with a peddler friend, he would always cross to the other side of the street when his friend began to peddle. One time, though, the friend began to peddle before the deaf man could cross to the other side. Instead, the deaf man stared at the window display in order to remove himself symbolically, if not physically, from the peddling encounter.

DISCUSSION

Historically, the deaf have been discriminated against. They have been viewed as incapable of performing many tasks and at times have been treated as charity cases (Best, 1943). They are stigmatized (Goffman, 1963). Yet, the deaf see themselves in a different way. They recognize their own capabilities and believe that only their hearing loss differentiates them from the hearing. The deaf do not necessarily view their impairment as a loss. The deaf do not want charity and have opposed being given a tax exemption for their hearing loss (Furth, 1973). The deaf "disavow" (Davis, 1961) their deviance and helplessness. Yet, they feel that peddling serves only to reinforce that image to the hearing. It increases their stigmatization.

The deaf's irritation with the putatively high earnings of peddlers is rooted in the historical and personal circumstances of the deaf. The deaf have encountered job discrimination in hiring, promotion, and salaries.[6] Many deaf people do not change jobs because of their uncertainty as to whether they could find another job or how the new work conditions would be. Peddling is thus a *double insult*: the peddler's supposedly high earnings are greater than many deaf people's "hard-earned" wages, and the peddler is seen as helping to perpetuate the discriminatory conditions in which the deaf find themselves.

Peddling is deviant within the deaf community only because the community is an outsider one. The deaf are not preoccupied daily with their outsider status. Yet, they realize that hearing people are dominant. The hearing control important aspects of deaf people's lives such as education and jobs.

In securing work, the deaf often must have connections: parents, hearing siblings, or friends. Once given a chance, they are on trial until they prove their abilities. Though hearing people also face this situation, they do not face it to the extent that the deaf do. As I noted in Chapter 1, the deaf are often underemployed in positions below their capabilities. Advancement usually ceases when a supervisory position is approached because the deaf are felt to be lacking the "essential" oral-aural skills necessary for such positions. They cannot use the telephone. Hearing workers who have been trained by the deaf are frequently promoted over those same deaf people to supervisory positions (Jones, 1969; Craig and Collins, 1970). Therefore, many deaf people are concerned with the hearing's perception of their willingness and ability to work.

The well-educated deaf, who have the most contact with the hearing either through professional employment or by being members of advisory organizations, are the most concerned about the hearing's perception of the deaf. As appointed or self-perceived spokespeople, they are often the moral entrepreneurs (Becker, 1963) of the community. They help to organize the already existing opposition within the deaf community toward peddling. Through education and exhortation they may even attempt to create such sentiment. Yet opposition within the community is not entirely dependent upon their actions.

Not too surprisingly, begging among the blind seems to be similar in its significance for blind people to the significance of peddling for the deaf community (Scott, 1969a). Many blind people resent and oppose begging because it presents a negative image of the blind to the sighted. In displaying the attitudes of helplessness, obeisance, and humility, blind beggars reinforce the sighted's stereotypical response to the blind—a response which among early Hebrews dictated that begging be the blind's role (Lemert, 1951).

Less obviously, "Uncle Tomism" within the black community is similar to peddling among the deaf. Uncle Tomism and blacks' reaction to "tomming" is complicated. Some

blacks may admire sophisticated and cunning Uncle Tom-
mers, whose "aggressive meekness" deludes whites to black
people's advantage. Typically, though, Uncle Tomism is repu-
diated by blacks (Pettigrew, 1964; Thompson, 1974). Both
Uncle Tomism and peddling perpetuate negative images
which neither blacks nor the deaf want accepted by the larger
society.[7] The self-pride of each outsider group is damaged
and their perceived rightful place in society is jeopardized.[8]

CONCLUSION

Peddling and the reaction to it within the deaf community
suggests that behavior which jeopardizes the outsiders' desired relationship with the wider society is often considered
deviant. Outsiders do not necessarily desire to abandon their
identity as outsiders. In fact, many are striving to strengthen
it. As I noted in the previous chapters, members of the deaf
community are committed to their way of life even as they
deal with their remaining ambivalence about who they are.
However, the deaf and other outsiders are concerned with the
image that the larger world has of them. Years and even
centuries of being placed and kept in an inferior position are
not easily forgotten. Therefore, behavior of fellow outsiders
which is seen as lending support to that subjugated position
becomes deviant. Such behavior spoils the collective identity
of the outsiders and jeopardizes their chances to be rightfully
included in activities controlled by the larger society.
    Although there are dissenting views (Hirschi, 1973), soci-
ologists have recognized that deviance may be functional for
the group in which it occurs. The sanctioning of deviance
may enhance the cohesiveness of the group or serve as a
boundary-maintaining device (Durkheim, 1960, 1966; Simmel, 1955; Coser, 1956; Dentler and Erikson, 1959; Scott,
1976). Without deviance, the "community would have no
inner sense of identity and cohesion, no sense of the contrasts which set it off as a special place in the larger world"
(Erikson, 1964: 15). The acts, though, may be deviant because they are perceived by the community of outsiders as

maintaining the symbolic boundary between themselves and the wider society. Such is the case for peddling among the deaf.

NOTES

1. Street people who work at marginal occupations are often keen observers of others. They must be in order to survive. For example, female beggars in Dublin have developed strategies involving appearance, speech, and the presence of infants in order to increase their earnings (Gmelch and Gmelch, 1978). The same can be said of successful criminals, who must be sensitive to social conventions (Letkemann, 1973).

2. Members of a gay community in California voiced similar concerns about being judged by the behavior of a few gays. As one member said:

I think it's too bad that so much of the world judges all gay people and all gay kids, both girls and guys, by a few of the social deviants that, you know, throw a bad light on all of us (Warren, 1974: 131).

3. In one episode of a highly rated comedy television show about the police, a detective arrested a beggar. The detective justified the arrest to his captain by arguing that the beggar was in good health. If the beggar were blind or deaf or all crippled up then that would be OK. However, the detective felt that this beggar was taking business from guys who needed it. If the beggar had a limp at least . . . Thus, the mass media present the image that deafness is a legitimate reason for peddling.

4. Even the peddling author implicitly acknowledges that peddling plays on the sympathy of the hearing. He notes that, for most people, "buying a card from the deaf is an opportunity for the buyer to feel real good inside" (Long, 1978: 6).

5. The peddling author argues that it is peddlers' boasts which lead to the mistaken idea that a day's work can earn a great deal of money (Long, 1978).

6. Due to various factors, the median income of the deaf is less than the median income of the U.S. population (Schein and Delk, 1974).

7. In a similar fashion, among Jewish students at eastern universities one may be called a "JAP," a Jewish American Princess, or sometimes Prince, for fitting the stereotypical image of Jews as overly concerned with money, ambition, success, and conspicuous consumption (Butler, 1979).

8. Pettigrew (1964: 46-47) argues, however, that the vigorous repudiation of "Uncle Tomism" by young blacks is suspicious, as if they were denying that behavior within themselves. Opposition to peddling may also be the result of some deaf people denying similar behavior in themselves. Many college-educated deaf attended school through funds provided by their state department of vocational rehabilitation. Jacobs (1974: 65) speaks of a "gimme" attitude among the deaf: Many services have been given to deaf individuals without their having to work for it. Consequently, some take for granted that anything is theirs for the asking. Some deaf individuals, therefore, may be denying their own "gimme" attitude in opposing deaf peddling. Thus ambivalence is again an important aspect of the deaf community.

5

STIGMA

Outsiders are typically characterized by the larger social world as different, odd, strange, or other than normal. They talk with a peculiar accent. They have the "wrong" skin color. They look different. They are ignorant. They cannot be trusted, and so on. According to Adam (1978), the composite portrait of Jews, blacks, and gays present these three groups of outsiders as "animals"—brutish, foul-smelling people—who are flamboyant, overly visible, hypersexual individuals who will corrupt others. Outsiders are stigmatized. As used by Erving Goffman (1963), the term "stigma" refers to a deeply discrediting trait. It may also be called a failing, a shortcoming, or a handicap. People develop assumptions about what other people should be like, about the kinds of characteristics they should possess. Those who create and control the larger social world develop assumptions about how others should appear, behave, and think. Yet, some people are found not to measure up to the standards which have been set. Each of these people who fall short become "reduced in our minds from a whole and usual person to a tainted, discounted one" (Goffman, 1963: 3). Thus, criminals, ethnic Americans, homosexuals, and other outsiders are stigmatized. Once stigmatized, they may be avoided, ridiculed, punished, or reacted to in numerous ways which indicate that they are less than fully human. The physically disabled are routinely stigmatized. In a society which cherishes youth, the physical abilities which typically accompany youth and good health, the impaired are looked down upon. People typically expect that

> those they confront on a daily basis will "appear to be normal."
> They will walk normally, speak intelligently, not have sight or
> hearing impaired, have the usual level of physical stamina, and be
> able to follow the train of a normal conversation with relative
> ease. Any alteration in these attributes leads others to define
> these individuals in less than positive terms [Lindesmith et al.,
> 1975: 535].

The physically disabled do not measure up to the standards set by the nondisabled. Being stigmatized, they have been singled out for special attention.

While there are many exceptions, the disabled have historically been treated as inferior by the nondisabled.[1] In ancient Sparta and Athens, malformed babies were exposed on a mountainside to die (Bender, 1970). Controversy continues today as to whether grossly deformed infants should be allowed to survive. Wealthy individuals and royalty often kept physically deformed or mentally impaired people as fools or jesters for the amusement of their guests. Such practices continue today in a slightly different but similar manner in the side shows or "freak" shows of traveling circuses and carnivals. Physical impairments have traditionally been viewed as an indication of the disabled's sin or their parents' sin and were both a means of punishment and of atonement (Hanks and Hanks, 1948; Meyerson, 1948; Oberman, 1965). Attitudes toward the disabled are typically less favorable than attitudes toward the nondisabled. For example, children prefer other children without impairments to those who are impaired (Richardson et al., 1961). Jokes about the physically disabled are more deprecating than jokes about other groups, such as salesmen or judges (Barker et al., 1953). The physically and mentally disabled are routinely portrayed in the mass media as bizarre and dangerous and are associated with acts of violence and hate (Bogdan and Biklen, 1977). In a parallel manner, "inferiorized" groups, such as black Americans, gays, and Jews, are portrayed in terms of "crime, immorality, disorder, or ugliness" (Adam, 1978: 32). Recent federal legislation such as the Rehabilitation Act of 1973, which prohibits discrimination based solely on a disability, is testimony to the fact that such discrimination has been widespread (Bogdan and Biklen, 1977). In much the same way that blacks have been the objects of racism and women of sexism, the disabled have been the objects of "handicapism" (Bogdan and Biklen, 1977). What has been said of the disabled in general can be said of the deaf in particular (see Chapter 1).

Everyday encounters between the physically disabled and the nondisabled are typically strained, inhibited, and awkward (Ladieu et al., 1948; Wright, 1960; Davis, 1961; Freidson, 1966; Kleck et al., 1966; Richardson, 1969; Sagarin, 1975). Often there is uncertainty or lack of agreement as to how the disability should be handled. Should it be recognized or left unnoticed? Should help be offered to the disabled (Ladieu et al., 1947)? Can they be included in various activities? The nondisabled are often curious, full of pity, or studiously nonchalant. They may fail to grant the disabled the respect and the regard which the disabled believe that their other attributes entitle them to. While the nondisabled may feel uncomfortable during and after encounters with the disabled, the disabled are often left with the distinct impression that they are somewhat less than normal. The disabled, though, may resist their stigmatization. Through various techniques they cope with imputations that their identities are spoiled (Davis, 1961; Voysey, 1972; Levitin, 1975).

In a world of sounds, the ability to hear and speak normally is highly valued. Those abilities are usually taken for granted. However, those who are outsiders in that world are not taken for granted. They are viewed as different or odd.

Their world without sound is not quite comprehensible. Hearing people wonder what it is like not to hear others' voices. More romantically, they wonder what it is like not to hear the singing of birds or the wind rustling through a tree. They pity the deaf, especially children who are deaf.[2] The lament is: "What will become of these poor children who are deaf?" In short, the deaf are stigmatized.

In this chapter I examine five specific issues in the stigmatization of the deaf: the *discrediting* of the deaf through their signing, deafness as a *master status,* the issue of *spread, scrutinization* from the larger hearing world, and *acceptance* in everyday encounters. These issues concern not only the deaf, but other outsiders as well. However, unlike many other outsiders, the deaf are physically impaired. That impairment profoundly disrupts communication with the hearing. For this reason, these issues of stigmatization are likely to be particularly resistant to change. I will briefly discuss this point at the end of the chapter. In the following chapter I will examine it in detail.

THE DISCREDITED DEAF

Those who create and control the larger social world often focus on a particular characteristic of outsiders which they scorn and ridicule. That particular characteristic may be disparagingly exaggerated or mocked. Whites may emphasize how dark a black person is. Heterosexuals ridicule the supposedly limp wrist of gays and their "swishy" manner. Americans deride the "funny" accents of immigrants. The hearing often focus their attention on deaf people's signing.

As I mentioned in the previous chapters and as I will pursue further in the next chapter, deafness is a relatively invisible disability. Compared to an arm amputation or facial disfigurement, deafness is much less apparent. Deaf people look "normal." They often blend into the hearing world. To use Goffman's terms, they are discreditable and are not yet discredited. People who possess a stigma which is easily observable are discredited. Black Americans or the facially disfigured are discredited. Other stigmata are more hidden to view and only later may become apparent. People who posess these kind of stigmata are discreditable. An ex-convict, a homosexual, or a deaf person are discreditable. Their failings could become known. Signing makes deaf people visible. It makes them stand out in a hearing world. It makes them discredited.

Americans are relatively reserved in their body movements. Compared to people in other countries, they show little emotion and are not physically expressive. Therefore, the animated facial, hand, and body movements of the deaf sometimes alarm the hearing. As Alexander Graham Bell (1883: 43) noted in his support of the oral philosophy of educating the deaf,

> gesticulations [of the deaf] excite surprise and even sometimes alarm in ignorant minds. In connection with this subject I may say that as lately as 1857 a deaf-mute was shot dead in Alabama by a man who was alarmed by his gestures.

More routinely, though, signing simply attracts the attention of the hearing. At times it may distract them. A deaf woman who works at a post office explained:

> The hearing workers talk a lot, but when I start to sign to a deaf worker, the hearing people tell me to stop signing. They say I "talk" too much. They tell me that because of my expressions [gestures and signs] other hearing workers have to stop their work and watch. When other deaf postal workers sign, it doesn't bother the hearing workers.

Even to hearing people who are familiar with the deaf, particularly animated signing may attract their attention; they, in turn, bring this to the attention of the deaf.

The nondisabled often stare at those who are facially disfigured, have an amputation, are confined to a wheelchair, or are in some way visibly disabled (White et al., 1948). The same is true for signing among the deaf. When the deaf sign in

public, especially in an enclosed area where hearing people
congregate, they are often stared at and even made fun of.
Public transport terminals and restaurants seem to be promi-
nent places for such occurrences. A deaf man recalled that

> one time, he, his wife, and two deaf friends were dining in a
> restaurant. One of the deaf friends was well educated, with advanced
> degrees. They were signing to one another, and the waitress made
> fun of them by mimicking their signs and gestures. At the end of the
> meal, the well-educated deaf woman wrote a note to the waitress
> which explained in very sophisticated words that her behavior was
> rude. The waitress did not understand the note, and therefore some
> customers explained to her what it meant. The cashier was embar-
> rassed by the incident and insisted that the deaf people not pay for
> their meals.

Other deaf people complain that even some hearing people
who show an interest in learning signs do so only in order to
stigmatize the deaf. Some hearing people may only be interested in learning signs related to sexual behavior so they
might use these signs in a derogatory and mocking way
(Woodward, 1979).

Members of the deaf community have experienced stares,
laughter, and mimicking gestures for years. Many have grown
accustomed to it. The stigmatizing behavior of the hearing is
just a small part of their lives. Therefore, many no longer
bother to react overtly to such behavior. They ignore it in
silence. When one deaf couple dines in a restaurant, they
imagine that they have drawn a curtain between themselves
and the hearing people who stare at them. Unless deaf individuals speak intelligibly or write well, there is little they can
do in reaction to the offensive behavior of hearing people
except "make a scene" themselves. Thus, a low verbal deaf
man with poor speech ignores stares in a restaurant but walks
out if he feels that the waitress is deliberately making him
wait. Some kinds of offensive behavior cannot be effectively
dealt with, whereas other kinds can.

While outsiders in a hearing world have grown accustomed
to stares at their signing, those related to outsiders may not

be accustomed to such stares. Hearing parents of deaf children and hearing children of deaf parents may be self-conscious when they sign in public. In Chapter 3 I mentioned
this issue. In fact, some speakers may at first be self-conscious when they sign in public. Hearing parents may not
want others to know that their children are deaf. Remember
too that the oral philosophy has been dominant until recently. Children are often self-conscious anyway. They may be
particularly uncomfortable with the attention that is created
by their signing to their deaf parents. In either case, the
hearing parents and hearing children may sign to their deaf
family members less in public than they do in private. They
may not sign at all. Hearing parents who sign little in public
may slow the language development of their deaf children.
Hearing children who sign little in public may create uncertainty for their deaf parents. As I noted in Chapter 3, the
hearing child's self-consciousness leads deaf parents to doubt
whether they in fact having nothing to be ashamed of.

Members of the deaf community have become accustomed
to the stigmatizing behavior of hearing people even though
they do not like it. Some "wise" hearing people may not be
as patient. While the deaf may simply let the stares and
comments of the hearing pass or not even be aware of them
until later, "wise" hearing people may criticize such behavior.

A deaf woman and her hearing sister, who signs, were eating in a
restaurant. Other hearing diners stared at their signed conversation.
The sister "told off" the hearing people, who were shocked because
they thought both women were deaf.

While signing is often an indication of deafness, it is not
necessarily a completely accurate one. Hearing people do
sign, and some sign fluently. Hearing people, however, typically interpret signing as an indication of deafness. This leads
to occasions, like the one mentioned above, where a hearing
person is mistaken for being deaf and thus has the opportunity, as well as the resources (i.e., intelligible speech), to
"turn the tables" on the offending hearing people. Or hearing

people may whisper derogatory remarks to one another in the presence of presumably several signing deaf people, only to learn to their chagrin that one or more were "wise" hearing people. In a similar fashion, an American may derogate foreign-speaking individuals, only to learn that some speak and understand English quite well. Or a presumably "stupid" person or a child may understand all too well what has been said in his or her presence, though it was not intended for their ears.

Recent research suggests that disabled people are not stared at because they are stigmatized but because they are a novel stimulus, unfamiliar to the nondisabled, and therefore elicit stares (Langer et al., 1976). The signing of deaf people is unfamiliar to many hearing people. An animated conversation among deaf people is likely to be a novel stimulus to the hearing. Clearly, though, the mimicking gestures and ridicule of signing by the hearing is more than a reaction to a novel stimulus. Even the quiet curiosity and stares of the hearing are interpreted by the deaf as indications of stigmatization. The stigmatization of the deaf and the novelty of their signed conversations seem to combine to produce the curiosity and stares of the hearing. It is surely the stigmatization, though, which is more difficult for the deaf to adjust to.

It becomes increasingly clear why signing is such an important aspect of the deaf community and of deaf people's identity. Members of the deaf community have had to withstand the traditional desire of hearing educators to forbid signing in classes for the deaf. However, that desire has been replaced with an effort to change the nature of sign language, to make it similar to the structure of English. Some of the deaf have experienced the frustration of not being able to learn through the oral approach. Many remember as children being left out or not being completely informed of family matters. Their parents did not know how to sign or they were opposed to it. The deaf have also had to cope with the stares, ridicule, and laughter of the hearing public. Resistance to such behavior strengthens the importance of signing within the deaf community for the identity of deaf people. When freedom to engage in a particular behavior is threatened, individuals will attempt to restore that freedom (Brehm, 1966). By refusing to submit to the stares of hearing individuals or to the efforts of educators to change sign language, the deaf community asserts itself and proclaims its existence in a hearing world.

MASTER STATUS

Those who create and control the larger social world often treat the "failing" of outsiders as a master status (Hughes, 1945). It is the particular stigma, the failing, which organizes people's behavior toward outsiders, and not the individual characteristics of those outsiders. The individual characteristics are overlooked, while the "failing" is emphasized. Thus, a black engineer with a college degree may be just another black person to many whites. So, too, may a black grade school dropout be just another black. Being black is the master status. Consequently, the individual characteristics of blacks may be overlooked. Deafness is the master status for those outside the hearing world.

Related to the notion of master status is the concept of homogeneity. Not only does the larger social world emphasize the "failing" of the outsiders, but it also treats those with the same "failing" as if they were the same. The larger social world tends to be unaware of or to ignore the differences among outsiders. To paraphrase a famous saying, an outsider is an outsider is an outsider. The larger social world tends to deal with individual members of a group of outsiders on the basis of what the members of the group have in common, their stigma. Previous experiences with an outsider may be applied matter-of-factly to others who are similarly stigmatized. Or the larger social world deals with outsiders in terms of their general notions about or stereotypes of the outsiders. Ex-mental patients are seen as dangerous; gays are effeminate; and so on.

The hearing world regards deafness (and its visible indication, signing) as a master status. Hearing people often respond to the deaf based on common sense notions of what deaf people are like. They often are unaware of the individual characteristics of the deaf. Previous experience with deaf individuals may be applied to all who are deaf. That previous experience is often awkward and uncomfortable as I will explain in the next chapter. I examined one instance of this phenomenon of master status in the previous chapter, where I noted that just by virture of their hearing impairment, deaf people may be treated as if they were peddlers. As children, the master status of members of the deaf community was their hearing loss.

A young deaf man explained how, as a student at the state school for the deaf, when one deaf boy stole something from a local store, the store clerks were "on guard" when a group of boys from the school went into town because they were deaf.

And so it continues to be for members of the deaf community as adults:

A deaf woman, who is a keypunch operator by training, applied for a job at a company. The job was advertised in the newspaper. She was told that she would be called back when there was an opening. A week later the advertisement still appeared in the newspaper. The woman was upset and went back to the company. Finally she was hired. Later she learned that the company was reluctant to hire her because they had a deaf woman working for them who happened not to be very capable. The company was afraid that she, too, would not be suitable.

Again, a young deaf man explained that while he was a student at a hearing university,

he asked a hearing student in a nearby dorm room to make a telephone call for him. After talking with the deaf student for a short time, the hearing student remarked that he thought all deaf people had limited interests like the deaf student's deaf roommate who sometimes showed to hearing students football cards that are included in packages of bubble gum.

Outsiders in a hearing world do identify strongly with their fellow members of the deaf community. Deafness and its shared experiences are an important part of membership in deaf communities and of the members identities. Yet, the members may find it awkward when the hearing only emphasize their deafness to the exclusion of their other characteristics. The deaf see little difference between themselves and those who control the larger social world, the hearing. Again and again I was told that there were really no important differences between deaf people and hearing people. The only difference was that deaf people could not hear and some could not speak. As a deaf man explained when I asked how he thought about himself:

> Well, I would resist any label. I would like to be classified as a person who has a hearing handicap.

SPREAD

Additional (often negative) characteristics and limitations are attributed to outsiders, based on their original "failing." Not only do blacks fall short of being white, but additional negative characteristics are attributed to them: laziness, low mentality, lack of responsibility, and so on. The evaluation of the physically disabled tends to spread from the specific impairment to other capabilities and attributes (Wright, 1960). For example, a student confined to a wheelchair may be viewed as more conscientious but also as feeling more inferior and being more unhappy than those not so confined (Wright, 1960). The same holds true for those considered deviant. Additional characteristics are attributed to them, based on their offensive behavior. Political radicals may be seen as ambitious, aggressive, stubborn, and dangerous (Simmons, 1965). A cluster of negative traits and not just the original "failing" is used to characterize outsiders (Goode, 1978).

Negative evaluations of the deaf spread from their hearing

impairment to their mental abilities. These generalizations of the hearing imply little sense and skill, and recall the term "deaf and dumb." As I noted in Chapter 1, the deaf have historically been viewed as incompetent to various degrees. Although the term "dumb" meant speechless or mute, it clearly connoted being senseless as well. A major journal in the field of deafness incorporated the term "dumb" in its title until the 1880s. As children, members of the deaf community most often faced the taunts of "deaf and dumb." As adults, though, they continue to face this additional negative attribution of the hearing. A deaf man in his sixties recalled that

> years ago, as a young adult, he and some deaf friends were on the El. After watching the deaf people, a hearing man wrote a note and handed it to one of them. The note was passed among the deaf people and finally reached him. It read, "Can you read and write English?" The young deaf man wrote, "No. Can you?" It was passed back to the hearing man who read it and looked dumbfounded.

The deaf man explained to me that hearing people often look at deaf people as if they were "animals" who can neither read nor write.

While the above incident happened years ago, similar ones occur frequently today, though perhaps in more subtle ways.

> As a young deaf couple was leaving their vacation hotel, the porter gave them their bill and then told them how much to tip him. The couple felt that the porter's action was a "little too much."[3]

Even deaf individuals who are known to be well educated by the hearing may still be treated as if they were not. A deaf teacher explained:

> There was a statewide workshop for teachers of the deaf at the University of California in Santa Barbara one summer. There Mrs. Jacobs and I ran into two charming young ladies who teach day classes in small towns. Since Mrs. Jacobs possesses all the oral skills in the family, she intercepted the conversational ball and

kept it passing back and forth. However, the inevitable impasse occurred; my wife failed to make the ladies understand what she was saying, so she turned to me and asked me to write down what she was trying to say. I complied, and handed the pad to one of the ladies. You can imagine my surprise and discomfort when she exclaimed. "You have perfect language. I don't have to correct a single thing!" [Jacobs, 1974: 43].

Deafness is the disability, not senselessness. Yet deaf people are often treated as if they were "deaf and dumb."

Even if hearing people realize that "dumb" refers to being mute, actions based on the assumption that deaf people are necessarily mute, may create momentary discomfort for those who are not.

A young deaf woman was hospitalized while awaiting an operation. The nurse placed a card on her chart which read, "This patient is deaf and mute." The woman, who has intelligible speech, indignantly cut off the last part of the card, which said that she was mute.

Not all deaf people are mute, which, as we shall see in the next chapter, may help to confuse encounters between the deaf and hearing.

Some deaf speak unnaturally, without "normal" voice quality and inflection. Negative characteristics may be attributed to these members of the deaf community based solely on their speech. Physical impairments, though, are an ambiguous predictor of other characteristics and capabilities (Davis, 1961). A hearing counselor remarked of a hearing-impaired woman:

I had a girl who called on the phone and I pictured her as big, unkempt, as fat as a slob. Her voice would just drive you up the wall. Gravel Gerdy had nothing compared to what this voice was. When I met her, she was a petite, very attractive woman of about 37.

The negative characteristics which are attributed to the deaf based on their speech may also recall the term "deaf and dumb." A deaf woman explained that

> her first husband, a hearing man, told her not to talk to him while they were out in public. The husband felt that her voice was high-pitched and sounded like a retarded person's voice.

Though false attributions can be made of anyone, the deaf are likely to experience them due to their "unnatural" speech. Because the oral philosophy of education has been historically so strong, some members of the deaf community remain sensitive to how their speech sounds to others. As I noted in Chapter 3, if they feel that their speech is irritating to hearing people, some deaf choose not to speak, even though their speech is intelligible. Characteristics falsely attributed to the deaf because of their speech will be taken up again from a different perspective in the next chapter.

SIZING UP THE OUTSIDER

Outsiders are often scrutinized by those who create and control the larger social world. Because they are seen as different or odd, their actions may be watched closely. The larger social world is waiting for them to "trip up," to make mistakes which confirm the fact that the larger social world assumes it already knows—that outsiders are not quite normal. Outsiders are inspected in order to see if they "measure up" to the task. Scrutinization often occurs on the job for the deaf, when they are given a trial period in order to determine if they can handle the work. One deaf woman asked for a nonpaid trial period in order to be given the opportunities to demonstrate her abilities. While trial periods are not uncommon for any worker, they occur frequently for the deaf and other outsiders because these people are stigmatized and their abilities are in doubt.

Scrutinization of outsiders is likely to be especially intense when the outsiders plan to marry members of the larger social world. Years of research show that the more intimate the contact desired by outsiders, the more vehemently they will be opposed by the larger social world (Simpson and Yinger, 1972). Blacks living two blocks away may be tolerated, but a black marrying one's white child is an entirely different situation. White parents closely inspect their prospective black son-in-law. Protestant parents size up their future Catholic daughter-in-law. Parents are often bewildered and angry when their children plan to marry "one of them."[5]

Relatively few deaf people marry hearing individuals. Less than 15% of those who became deaf before the age of 19 marry a person with normal hearing (Schein and Delk, 1974). When they do, however, they may be closely scrutinized by the hearing partner's family. A deaf man "fondly" recalled what happened thirty-five years ago when his hearing fiancee told her family that they were to be married:

> Her mother hit the roof, and came down on the next train, and [I] had to go in hiding because she was so angry about it. She didn't accept the situation until it had been agreed for me to talk with the elders of the family, her [the fiancée's] uncles. They couldn't find anything wrong with me except I was deaf [laughter]. So her mother had to drop her objections.

Parents, though, may not drop their objections. They may continue to be resentful toward their children and the outsiders whom their children have married. A young deaf woman who is married to a hearing man explained that

> her husband's parents were firmly against their being married. They told him it would last only six months, but it has lasted ten years. The couple was forced to elope out of state because the groom was under age, without parental consent, and the groom's sister refused to sign the wedding license. Ten years later, the deaf woman, now a mother, still feels that she is not accepted by her husband's parents.

Couples involved in mixed marriages—between outsiders and those who are not outsiders—may find themselves unwelcomed by the family and friends of the partner who is not an outsider. However, they may also find themselves unwelcomed by the community of outsiders. Blacks who marry whites may be shunned or ridiculed by the black community as well as by the white community (Day, 1972). Jewish parents typically assume that their child will marry a Jew and may become distraught if they do not (Simpson and Yinger, 1972). In marrying outside his or her own group, the outsider and the one who is not an outsider have cast at least a slight doubt on the importance of each group's identity. Their marriage indicates that the world does not end at the boundary of each group. This particular issue needs to be investigated further with respect to the deaf community.

While it is not surprising that deaf people are scrutinized by the hearing parents of their hearing fiancé(e), they may also have to contend with the reservations of hearing parents of a hearing impaired fiancé(e). Unlike racial or ethnic outsiders, for example, deaf people typically have parents who are not outsiders. The same would be true for many other physically disabled outsiders. As I noted in Chapter 2, less than 10% of deaf people have deaf parents. Hearing parents may desire that their deaf child marry someone who is not deaf. This situation would very roughly correspond to a white couple's desire that their adopted black child marry a white person. Yet most black children's and most other outsiders' parents are also outsiders. Therefore, this particular conflict is not as likely to arise for those outsiders whose parents are similarly stigmatized as it is for the deaf.

A deaf wife explained that

> when she was dating her deaf husband, her hearing parents wondered if her boyfriend were hard of hearing. They hoped that he was. She told them no. He was deaf. Now, though, her parents "love him like a son."

Even if parents finally accept their child's marrying an outsider, concern grows once more when grandchildren are born. The typical grandparents' concerns over the sex of the child, whose side of the family the child takes after, and so

on are replaced by one overriding question. To what extent
will the grandchild be an outsider too? What will be the skin
color of the child of a black-white marriage? How will the
grandchild of a Protestant-Catholic marriage be brought up?
Whose customs will the offspring of a Chicano-Anglo marriage follow? Parents who have sons or daughters, but perhaps especially in-laws who are outsiders, may worry if their
grandchildren will be outsiders too.

Hearing parents of deaf children or of those who marry
deaf individuals are concerned that their grandchildren not be
deaf. The same holds true for other disabilities as well.
Usually the children are not deaf, though. Of the children
born to couples where at least one spouse is deaf, 88% have
normal hearing. That figure decreases to 81% when both
parents are congenitally deaf (Schein and Delk, 1974: 45).
Yet, the uncertainty always exists. It may even linger on for
months or even years after the child is born. This is so
because deafness is often difficult to detect in early infancy.
A deaf mother with intelligible speech and a great deal of
residual hearing explained that

> her parents had expected her to marry a hearing man. She did not.
> When the first child was found to be deaf at 8 months of age from
> an infection, her parents took it very hard. Was the child deaf? They
> did not think so. At age 2, her parents felt acupuncture should be
> tried in order to restore their grandchild's hearing. The deaf husband
> felt that there was no need for that. He was proud of his child. It
> made no difference that the child was deaf. Now, several years and
> several deaf children later, the wife's parents sign, to which they had
> long been opposed. They sign because their grandchildren are deaf.

The hope remains among members of the larger social world,
though, that even if one's child or in-law is an outsider,
maybe the grandchildren will not be.[6]

ACCEPTANCE

According to Goffman (1963: 8-9), the central feature of
stigmatized people's lives is the issue of acceptance. Do other

people give the stigmatized individual the respect "which the uncontaminated aspects of his social identity have led him to anticipate receiving?" The answer is often no. Outsiders are first and foremost treated as tainted people and only later, if ever, as just people. As a visibly injured respondent noted in research thirty years ago:

> You can't write an article about it. It can be said in one sentence—there is no acceptance [Ladieu et al., 1948: 55].

As I observed in Chapters 2 and 3 and earlier in this chapter, members of the deaf community have faced taunts and teasing, ridicule and neglect all their lives. The lack of social acceptance in the hearing world is pervasive. While members of the deaf community may not like it, it is something that they have grown accustomed to. However, when directly communicating with the hearing, members are concerned with a specific issue: the willingness or reluctance of hearing people to repeat their spoken message. Members define this issue as involving social acceptance. In these focused encounters, the issue is difficult to avoid.

Unlike blacks, ethnic Americans, gays, and many other outsiders, the stigma which deaf people bear is also a very real physical impairment. As I will explore in the next chapter, deafness and its accompanying limitations often disrupt encounters between the deaf and the hearing. Here, I want to examine only one aspect of that difficulty which goes beyond a communication problem: the putative reluctance of many hearing people to repeat their spoken communication to the deaf. That reluctance is taken by the deaf as an indication that the hearing do not fully accept them as equals. What seems to be a communication problem has deeper significance for the deaf.

Even if deaf people are skilled lipreaders, they frequently do not understand a spoken message the first time they see it. Sometimes, of course, they never do. Repetition is needed and often asked for by the deaf, but sometimes not willingly given by the hearing. This seems to be a communication problem, and it is. Yet it also has a deeper significance for deaf people. A deaf woman explained that one time

a hearing co-worker spoke too fast for her to understand. She asked the woman to repeat, but the hearing worker became angry. The deaf woman asked how the hearing worker would feel if she, the deaf woman, signed too fast for the hearing worker (who had learned some signs from the deaf woman) to understand.

The need to have a spoken message repeated is not just a communication problem. Repeating a spoken message is a sign of willingness to deaf people to accept them for what they are—people with a hearing impairment who may happen to need the hearing's words repeated, no more and no less. Refusal or unwillingness to repeat a spoken message is taken by the deaf as an indication that the hearing person does not want to bother with them. If a person is fully accepted as an equal, then when that individual does not understand a spoken message, it is naturally repeated. Of course, sometimes the repetition is accompanied by good-natured ribbing which often takes the form of: "What are you deaf or something?" Deaf people realize this. Therefore, they interpret a refusal or unwillingness to repeat as a lack of social acceptance. They are not "normal" enough to be accorded the common courtesy of asking for and receiving repetition.

A deaf postal worker, thoroughly aware of this situation, explained it very clearly:

Sometimes hearing people don't want to take the trouble to repeat what they said to me if I didn't understand. The "kids" [young workers] at the post office are pretty good about repeating, but sometimes they don't want to bother either. That bothers me. If a hearing person didn't understand, then the other hearing person would repeat what he said. It's the same for a deaf person if they don't understand. But hearing people won't always repeat.

At times, even the hearing children of deaf parents will not repeat their message to their parents. However, hearing people may not see that it is the same for a deaf person as it is for a hearing person. Yet, that is part of the dynamics of the situation between outsiders and those who create and control the larger social world. If it were otherwise, then the deaf might no longer be outsiders.

CONCLUSION

Outsiders are stigmatized by those who create and control the larger social world. Particular behaviors or attributes of outsiders may be ridiculed or mocked. Their stigmata become their master statuses. Individual capabilities and characteristics are often ignored. The failings of outsiders are assumed to spread to other attributes as well. A cluster of negative characteristics are attributed to them. While limited contact with outsiders may be tolerated, more intimate contact is often closely inspected or resisted. Parents often balk when their child wishes to marry an outsider. Their concern rises again when grandchildren are born. Will they, too, be outsiders? All this characterizes the deaf. They are outsiders in a hearing world.

As I will discuss in the next chapter, deafness is not just a stigma; it is also an impairment which disrupts communication with the hearing. This has profound implications for reducing the stigmatization of the deaf. Much research on intergroup relations suggests that interaction between outsiders and members of the larger social world can reduce prejudice toward and stigmatization of outsiders. Pleasant, equal-status contact, contact in which outsiders and those who are not outsiders depend on one another to achieve a common goal, or where outsiders are seen in situations not usually associated with the prevalent stereotypes of them, best reduce prejudices. However, "incidental, involuntary, tension-laden contact is likely to increase prejudice" (Simpson and Yinger, 1972: 683). Contact which is "stylized, socially distant and unequal" will reinforce our stereotypes of outsiders, not diminish them (Gooden, 1978: 90).

However, encounters between the deaf and hearing is often strained, awkward, and confusing–typically impersonal and full of tension. Increased contact between the deaf and the hearing does not necessarily increase communication or understanding. Increased contact with the deaf may only lead to a minimal increase in knowledge about deafness (Furfey and Harte, 1964: 66-67). The hearing may be more bewildered after interacting with the deaf than before. They may have less positive attitudes after interacting with the deaf, rather than more positive ones (Emerton and Rothman, 1978). Unlike many other outsiders' "failings," deafness does inhibit interaction with the larger social world, regardless of whether the deaf are stigmatized or not.

NOTES

1. In some situations the disabled are viewed in a positive fashion (Wright, 1960). For example, in certain segments of the Brazilian population and in some African tribes, epileptics qualify for the prestigious position of witch doctor because of their symptoms (Safilios-Rothschild, 1970).

2. In the abstract. the hearing may have slightly positive or indifferent attitudes toward the deaf (Emerton and Rothman, 1978). The results of attitude surveys must be interpreted with caution. What is important are not the abstract attitudes of the hearing toward the deaf, but the reactions of the hearing toward the deaf in concrete situations.

3. One might argue that the deaf couple misinterpreted the actions of the porter who typically tells all the guests how much to tip him. While that is possible, it may also be irrelevant. More importantly, the incident suggests that occasions when hearing people treat the deaf as "dumb" are so frequent that the deaf are likely to interpret possible occasions of that treatment as actual occasions.

4. The mass media may help perpetuate the image that the deaf are dumb. Newspaper and magazine articles which discuss the deaf still refer to them as deaf and dumb. The case of a made-for-television movie, *Dummy*, based on a book of the same name (Tidyman, 1974), is of interest here. Although an educator of the deaf was contacted by the author of the book and told the author that such a term was offensive to the deaf, the author felt that such a title was needed for and justified by its dramatic importance, as well as by the fact that the title character was called Dummy in real life (Kirchner, 1980). For similar reasons, the movie, *Fatso*, has drawn criticism from a national organization for overweight Americans. While few people would dream of entitling a film *Nigger*, "dummy" and "fatso"

are terms just as offensive to their respective stigmatized groups as "nigger" is to blacks. All three terms have been used to keep those groups in subordinate positions and are symbols of those subordinate positions.

5. See Simpson and Yinger (1972: ch. 16) for a discussion about interracial, interfaith, and interethnic marriages, and offspring of such marriages.

6. From the opposite viewpoint, outsider grandparents, too, are likely to be concerned with whether their grandchild will be like them, an outsider, or like those who monopolize reality, as black parents are concerned with the skin coloring of the offspring of a black-white marriage. Deaf grandparents must surely wonder if their grandchildren will understand what it means to be deaf, even though they do not wish that the grandchildren be deaf.

6

ENCOUNTERS WITH
THE HEARING

Outsiders are often characterized by the larger social world as odd, strange, or somehow other than normal. They are stigmatized. Consequently, encounters between outsiders and those who create and control the larger social world are often strained, inhibited, and awkward. In the previous chapter I examined the stigmatization of the deaf. Stigmatization, though, cannot fully explain the interaction between the deaf and the hearing. Unlike gays, ethnic Americans, and many other outsiders, the deaf are physically impaired. And like other outsiders who are physically disabled, their impairment and its accompanying limitations may disrupt encounters with those who are not disabled. These disruptions, however, are unrelated to whether the deaf are viewed as odd or not.

Encounters between the disabled and the nondisabled are often strained due to the impairments themselves and how they are managed. Certain features of a blind-sighted encounter can only be understood as the result of the strain that a visual impairment may create for the interaction. Blindness may interfere with establishing the interactants' identities and may create communication problems for both the blind and sighted (Scott, 1969a, 1969b). A wheel-

chair-bound individual may find that it is difficult to keep up
with normally mobile companions on the sidewalk and into
and through buildings. Similar problems occur for those with
heart trouble or arthritis (Strauss and Glaser, 1975). Difficulty in muscle control and abnormality in appearance may
interfere with face-to-face communication because facial and
body gestures may convey unintended information (Richardson, 1969). Therefore, stigmatization is only one issue which
can spoil interaction between the disabled and the nondisabled—in this case, between the deaf and the hearing.
Impairments, though, are not necessarily disruptive or
limiting. Whether they are disruptive or not depends on the
specific situation (Wright, 1960). Blindness does not interfere
with telephone conversations, but it may disrupt face-to-face
encounters, as mentioned above. Disabilities are disruptive in
certain situations when they *cause the assumptions and related routine practices which usually successfully maintain
interaction in those situations to become problematic.* A
breach in the taken-for-granted interactional order has occurred. Coping strategies used by both the disabled and the
nondisabled are attempts to compensate for those assumptions and practices which this time have failed.

ORIENTATION

The societal reaction or labeling perspective in sociology
emphasizes a long-neglected aspect of deviance—the assess-
ment and reaction of others to the putative deviant. It calls
our attention to the accusers and not only to those accused
(Becker, 1974). According to the societal reaction approach,
the key to understanding the physically disabled is not their
impairment, but the nondisabled's reaction to it (Safilios-
Rothschild, 1970: 115). Consequently, stigmatization has
been emphasized in explaining the often awkward encounters
between the disabled and the nondisabled. Yet the nondisableds' reactions are not merely to the disableds' putatively
spoiled identities. Rather, the reactions also arise out of the
assumptions and routine practices which usually successfully

maintain interaction. Therefore, the reactions of the nondisabled are important in understanding the physically disabled,
but in more complex ways than the societal reaction perspective has so far suggested.

Further, disabled people's primary concern, as it is for the
nondisabled, is often to accomplish everyday activities. Managing their putatively spoiled identities is not always an issue.
When ordering a meal in a restaurant, making purchases in a
store, crossing the street, or navigating into and through
buildings, disabled people are not necessarily concerned with
managing their stigmata. Therefore, strategies which the disabled use to facilitate interaction with the nondisabled may
reveal rather than conceal their impairments. Canes and guide
dogs identify the blind as visually impaired, but they also aid
the blind's mobility. The disabled may even use strategies
which imply that they are more impaired then they in fact
are. Thus, coping strategies used by the disabled cannot be
fully understood within the framework of stigmatization.

In this chapter, I analyze the often awkward and confusing
interaction which occurs in short-term, usually mundane, and
typically impersonal encounters between the deaf and the
hearing. Interaction between a clerk and a customer is such
an encounter. Interaction between the deaf and the hearing is
often disrupted due to the impact of the impairment and of
its accompanying limitations on social interaction. Once
those disruptions have been identified, I examined how the
deaf in particular, but also the hearing, cope with them. We
must move beyond the concept of stigma in order to understand fully the everyday lives of deaf people. Yet, in order to
understand how deafness and its accompanying limitations
disrupt interaction with the hearing, we need to examine the
assumptions and routine practices of the hearing world.

CONVERSATION

As I mentioned in Chapter 1, much of human interaction
is based on the assumption that people can hear and speak.
We communicate through telephones, radios, television, inter-

com systems, and loudspeakers. Warning signals are often buzzers, sirens, or alarms. Time is structured by bells and whistles. And people talk. In conversation, which "assumes an easy exchange of speaker-hearer role", strain occurs between the deaf and the hearing (Goffman, 1974: 498). An easy exchange of the speaker and hearer roles requires competence in the language used (Chomsky, 1965). It also requires competence in the norms and forms of interaction that the ethnographers and ethnomethodologists of communication have investigated—turn taking, whom to address, when to talk, what style of speech to use, and so on (Schegloff, 1968; Bauman and Sherzer, 1974; Hymes, 1974; Schiffrin, 1977). People typically must also be able to hear and speak, though not necessarily, as I explain later. Inadequate performances at each level of competence can inhibit conversation.

As I demonstrate throughout this chapter, interaction between foreigners and natives resembles in many ways encounters between the deaf and the hearing. Those who are foreigners in a country are typically outsiders in that country as well. Both the deaf and foreigners share a common problem, communication. And it is partly their communication problems which lead to their being outsiders. Therefore, the assumptions and routine practices which I examine for hearing and speaking seem to occur at other levels of competence involved in performing hearing and speaking *roles*—for example, linguistic competence.

Strain in encounters between the deaf and the hearing is due to the impact of deafness and of its accompanying limitations on conversation.[1] The effects of deafness on conversation are fully realized within the assumptions and routine practices of hearing people. These assumptions and practices usually successfully maintain interaction. Yet they often lead to confusion when applied to encounters with the deaf.

NOTHING UNUSUAL IS HAPPENING

People typically initiate interaction with the assumption that "nothing unusual is happening" (Emerson, 1970). Even in problematic situations, we often act as if nothing is out of the ordinary. Only under certain circumstances are we likely to recognize that "something unusual is happening" (Emerson, 1970; 219-220). Such is the case in encounters between the deaf and the hearing. Hearing people typically assume that everyone can competently hear and speak. As an extension of that assumption, hearing people often infer that those who speak must be able to hear. Hearing and speaking are seen as naturally going together. Therefore, those who cannot hear may be viewed as unable to speak. These assumptions lead to awkward and confused encounters between the deaf and the hearing in two major ways.

First, the assumptions lead hearing people to overlook the very real limitations in the hearing abilities of deaf people. By literally assuming "more than meets the eye," hearing people make false attributions about whom they are interacting with. These mistaken attributions lead hearing people to act in inappropriate ways, given the limitations of the deaf.

Second, the stance that nothing unusual is happening is not always maintained. It sometimes crumbles when confronted by the disconfirming actions of the deaf. It sometimes is merely discarded when it is recognized as inappropriate. In either case, something unusual *is* happening which hearing people are rarely prepared for. As I will discuss later, participants may even have different ideas of what it is that is unusual. There should be little wonder, though, that the hearing are not prepared. Deafness is a relatively low-prevalence disability (Schein and Delk, 1974). Therefore, most hearing people have little experience with the deaf. Further, hearing people often assume that nothing unusual is happening, even when that is not the case (e.g., they have encountered a deaf person without realizing it). The stance that nothing unusual is happening, as well as the imputation that something unusual is happening, concerns both the hearing and speaking abilities of people and the interplay between the two.

Hearing

To point out the obvious, hearing people rarely initiate a conversation with the inquiry as to the other person's hearing ability. Though hearing people know that some people are deaf, they do not routinely act as if that were the case. Because deafness is an invisible impairment, interacting with a deaf person does not necessarily reveal the person's deafness. Deaf people can literally become victims of the assumption that everyone can hear:

Deaf-Mute Found Fatally Shot

A deaf-mute was found shot to death Friday in which police believe was a killing prompted by the victim's inability to hear and obey a robber's demands. [Chicago Sun Times, May 31, 1975: 5]

The robber assumed that his victim could hear, and this assumption led him to misframe (Goffman, 1974) the actions of the deaf man. The deaf-mute was treated as an uncooperative hearing person rather than as a deaf person who temporarily could not cooperate. Equally dramatic mistakes occur when deaf children are diagnosed as mentally ill or mentally retarded rather than recognized as deaf. The inability to respond to spoken directions and commands is taken as an indication of retardation or mental illness (Vernon, 1969). No doubt these mistakes are becoming less prevalent as psychiatric and psychological diagnoses become more sophisticated.

A more common instance may occur in a supermarket when a deaf person inadvertently blocks the aisle. The deaf shopper does not hear the approach of the hearing customer, the muted noises of impatience, or the request to move aside. Again, the deaf person is treated as an uncooperative hearing person.

Hearing people who know that the deaf person is impaired may nevertheless routinely act as if that were not the case. Deaf people may be conversing, however awkwardly, with a sales clerk when the clerk casually turns and involves other store personnel in the transaction. Such behavior is common and is not meant to nor does it exclude a *hearing* customer from what is happening. Yet, the store clerk's routine action for hearing customers effectively excludes deaf customers from being informed. Or a sales clerk may matter-of-factly ask for the telephone number of a deaf customer who is paying with a check. However, many deaf people do not own telephones. Again, though, the ability to hear and/or the accounterments of it are routinely taken for granted.[2]

Even hearing people who are acquainted with a deaf individual, friends, co-workers, or team members, may momentarily overlook that the individual is deaf. This seems to occur especially in gatherings of several hearing people. A deaf man recalled his involvement with a group of hearing individuals:

> The group was politically aware and very argumentative. Arguments, discussions become so heated that they'd just about forget me. I would be left out. All the time that I was left out, they didn't mean to leave me out. It was just circumstances. So that the social involvement with them was not very successful from my point of view.

Foreigners who do not know the native language well may find themselves in similar situations.

The stance that nothing unusual is happening is maintained due to several factors. Deafness is an invisible impairment. Except through self-disclosure, signing, display of a hearing aid, or inability to appropriately respond to auditory stimuli, hearing people may not realize that the person they have encountered is deaf. Even those potential cues are ambiguous and can be misinterpreted. Thus, deaf people look "normal." Routinely they unintentionally pass as hearing. This ambiguity makes it easier to assume that nothing is out of the ordinary (Emerson, 1970: 218). Further, to abandon that stance may require a more complex performance than to maintain it (Emerson, 1970: 219). For example, to overlook that one person in a group is deaf is much easier than continually to interrupt the conversation in order to make sure that the deaf person is completely informed. Finally, as I will discuss later, coping strategies that deaf people use may present the impression that little or nothing is out of the ordinary or may be interpreted by hearing people as such.

In other situations where the encounter between the deaf and the hearing is more direct and focused, the assumption that everyone can hear may crumble as hearing people repeatedly fail to make themselves understood and deaf people fail to understand them. As I will discuss later, the deaf cope with this potential problem through different strategies.

Once hearing people recognize that their interactional partner is deaf, they may bring a further assumption to bear on the encounter. Hearing people are often amazed at how well deaf people speak or that they speak at all. This amazement is not unfounded, since people typically learn to speak by hearing and then imitating the speech of others. Further, it creates no special problems, though it may create some embarrassment. However, when the underlying assumption on which it is based is taken to its extreme, then it does create a problem.

Hearing people sometimes act as if deaf people cannot speak, at least not intelligibly. Though infrequent, this stance dates back to Aristotle's conclusion that those born deaf were also speechless (Bender, 1970). As one deaf man, whose speech, though not "perfect," was easily understandable to me, explained:

> Point is, that a lot of my problems come from the fact that even though I had pretty good speech people were deaf to me if they found out I was deaf. It seemed that psychologically their finding out that I'm deaf made them decide that they were not going to understand me when I spoke to them and that gave me a lot of frustration and embarrasment.

The deaf person's speech becomes unintelligible to the hearing listener only after the deafness has been disclosed.

Speaking

Hearing people start with the stance that everyone can talk. Some deaf people do have intelligible speech, but they still cannot hear. These deaf people find that if they talk to a hearing person they are spoken to as if they were hearing. The deaf individual may then disclose that they are deaf. Informing hearing people that one is deaf, though, may only elicit statements of "deaf and dumb" or visible indications that the hearing people are tense and do not know how to proceed.

However, because deafness is not immediately visible, hearing people may continue to act as if these deaf people who speak well are hearing, even though they declare their deafness.

> Everytime he [a deaf person] used his speech to place his request, the airline clerk would automatically answer orally, giving the necessary details which would most of the time contain numbers. The deaf man found that it was very easy to misread lips, and end up with reservations for wrong flights. Then he would have a very difficult time convincing the clerk that he could not hear and that it would be better for the clerk to jot down the needed information so that he could be 100 percent sure before confirming the reservation; the clerk could not understand that one who spoke so well could have a hard time understanding him in turn [Jacobs, 1974: 22].

Due to the ambiguity of the situation (i.e., the deaf person looks "normal" and speaks well), the stance that nothing unusual is happening may be maintained even in the face of disclaimers.[3]

Other deaf people with usable, if not "perfect," speech, have been mistaken for being German or English or African, if they were black, rather than recognized as being deaf. Not only were the deaf assumed to be hearing because of their serviceable speech, but an additional, mistaken characteristic was attributed to them.

Americans who speak a foreign language better than they understand it may encounter problems in that foreign country similar to those encountered at the airline ticket counter by the deaf man. Americans who telephone "Good morning!" in Spanish to a Mexican hotel clerk, order dinner in French in a Paris restaurmant, or say "Fill it up!" in German to a Munich gas station attendant may find that their interactional partners respond rapidly in their native languages. This may leave the Americans bewildered and chagrined. Because there were no other cues to the contrary, the Americans' brief performances as speakers led their foreign interactional partners to assume that they were competent hearers. Mistaken characteristics are often attributed to people based on their speech (Lambert et al., 1960; Kramer, 1963).

In other situations, though, the assumption that everyone can speak may not be maintained. Some deaf people cannot talk or their speech is unintelligible. Other deaf individuals' speech becomes intelligible only after hearing people have become familar with it. Several respondents noted that, at schools for the deaf, their teachers judged their speech to be good, but once they left school they had difficulty being understood. For example, a deaf woman orders hot chocolate but receives a hot dog instead. After learning English, foreigners may encounter similar problems.

Deaf people who do speak, though, cannot auditorily monitor their speech. What was meant for only a few people may be broadcast throughout the entire room. Or, because their speech has become inaudible, deaf speakers may find their hearing listeners staring with incomprehension. The deaf may mispronounce words without realizing it because the mistakes are not heard. This inability of deaf people to obtain the auditory feedback of their speech also leads to what might be called "deafisms."[4] During conversation or in reverie deaf people may emit strange vocal sounds, clicking noises, humming sounds, or grunts. Although they are unaware that they are producing such potentially distracting and disturbing noises, the result is to strain the interaction with the hearing.

COPING STRATEGIES

While encounters between the deaf and the hearing are often strained and confused, both parties usually attempt to complete the interaction successfully. The coping strategies used by both the deaf and the hearing are attempts to repair the breach in the taken-for-granted interactional order, to compensate for those assumptions and practices which have failed.

Deaf people are continually faced with these interactional problems, whereas any single hearing person may rarely encounter a deaf individual (Goffman, 1963). Consequently, the deaf are likely to have developed more effective strategies than have the hearing. Strategies used by the deaf may be practical, learned techniques developed over years of experience. The hearing, though, may base their strategies on "common sense." However, the strategies employed by the participants may be ineffective due to the same assumptions and practices which initially gave rise to the strain.

Here I want to focus primarily on the strategies used by the deaf. Strategies used by naive hearing people will be discussed to the extent that they interact with the strategies of the deaf. The deaf deal with potential conversational problems with the hearing in two major ways. One is to help maintain the hearing's orientation that nothing unusual is happening. The second way is openly to acknowledge that something is out of the ordinary and guide hearing people through the encounter. These two approaches relate both to hearing and speaking as well as to the interplay between the two. As I will mention throughout, similar strategies are used by other physically impaired people as well as by foreigners. In their own ways, of course, they too are outsiders.

Maintaining "Nothing Unusual is Happening"

Though the deaf have very real limitations in hearing and often in speaking, they may still attempt to perform the hearer and speaker roles. The general approach is to act in what would be an appropriate way if one could hear and speak. This general strategy is carried out through four specific techniques: *pretense; being alive* to the situation; *substitution* of senses; and *collusion* with "wise" hearing people. These techniques apply to performing the hearer and speaker roles, though some are more likely to be used in performing one role rather than the other. Some of the techniques may be used even when the impairment has been disclosed. Their important feature is not to conceal the deafness, though they may do that. Rather, they allow the interaction to proceed as if the person were not deaf.

Pretense. Some deaf individuals pretend that they understand the speaker's talk. The deaf smile in agreement, and the speaker may proceed unthinkingly. As one deaf man remarked, if the conversation is not that important, then he lets it pass. Yet the conversation could become important without his knowing it. If the speaker asks a question or expects a comment, awkward silence may predominate for both. The deaf individual's smiles and nods no longer suffice as appropriate responses.

Similar techniques are used by foreigners as well as by those with other physical impairments. Foreigners too may smile or nod their heads even if they do not fully understand what is being said. Visually impaired people who agree with their sighted friends' comments concerning a painting may be pretending in order to pass as sighted. Yet, pretense need not be used only to manage stigmatization.

In general, those who do not understand what is being talked about, even though they hear what is being said, often pretend to understand. For example, children, inadequately prepared students, and patients may often use this technique. In these situations pretense may be used because the individuals know less than what they would like others to believe. They are managing their stigmata of ignorance. The deaf, too, pretend at times in order to conceal the fact that they do not understand what is being said. Yet, pretense may also be the easiest way to conclude an unimportant conversa-

tion. Thus, a technique which seems to be a way of managing stigma may be used merely to accomplish everyday activities.
Being Alive. A related technique to pretense is to be alive to ordinary, routine features of situations that others take for granted. Goffman (1963: 88) notes that those who pass must often be alive to aspects of the situation that others do not attend to. Again, such a technique can serve a purpose different than stigma management. The deaf may be alert to cues other than auditory ones in order to act appropriately. When in a restaurant deaf people may not hear the waitress's request for their order. However, by noticing the waitress's approach and the position of her pencil and order pad, the deaf may appropriately respond as if such a request has been heard. Deaf customers who cannot hear how much their purchases cost or may position themselves in order to see the total on the cash register. Others may hand the cashier "enough" money to cover whatever the amount might be. Foreigners who use the latter technique may do so at the risk of being short-changed. Color-blind drivers are alive to features of traffic and traffic control that normally sighted drivers take for granted. By noting the position of the light and movements of the surrounding traffic, color-blind drivers can successfully negotiate intersections. In this case, being alive means staying alive.
Substitution of Senses. Deaf people may substitute one sense or modality of action for another in order to perform the hearer and speaker roles. This technique is most widely used and misunderstood in connection with the hearing role.
Some of the deaf attempt to perform the hearer role through lipreading. Lipreading, though, is often inadequate. Many speech sounds are indistinguishable on the speaker's lips (e.g., /b/ and /p/). Hearing people often talk through pursed lips or enunciate poorly. Facial hair of male speakers can obscure the visibility of their speech. Strangers are more difficult to lipread than those who are familiar (Pintner, 1929). Foreign accents make lipreading even more difficult. Finally, a gathering of several people poses multiple prob-

lems: Sight lines from the deaf person to the various potential speakers are not equally clear, and if they were, such an
arrangement would inhibit the interaction; it is difficult to
follow the talk as it moves from one speaker to another; and
the talk itself may be composed of simultaneous emissions
from several speakers.

Consequently, deaf people may silently sit in group situations or avoid them altogether if possible. Remember the
deaf bowler in Chapter 2. Some tell their hearing workers to
continue without them at the coffee break, while others may
occasionally ask, "What's going on?" As one deaf man, who
depended on a hearing aid, remarked:

> I don't go down for coffee with the others [hearing co-workers].
> In a group I can't follow what's going on; plus the noise, cups and
> silverware clanking. Maybe in a one to one or one to two
> [situation] I might take a break. When Pete Kelly was here, he's a
> hearing person who can sign, I used to go down with him. He
> could fill me in. If there was any confusion, I'd ask him, "What
> gives?"

A few deaf people may even try to show hearing people how
it feels to be left out.

> A deaf woman took a hearing co-worker to lunch with her and
> several deaf friends. The hearing worker felt left out, just as the deaf
> woman did when dining with the group of hearing workers. The deaf
> woman felt that the demonstration helped the hearing person to
> understand the situation from the deaf woman's viewpoint.

Thus, within a group of several learning people substitution
of senses may not be very effective.

Those deaf who do lipread must contend with the coping
strategies that many hearing people bring to the encounter
when they learn that their interactional partner is deaf.
Hearing people often exaggerate their mouth movements in
the well-intentioned but mistaken belief that such movements make it easier for the deaf person to read their speech.

Some, familiar only with the "hard of hearing" or using the "hard of hearing" as a model for the deaf, shout or move closer to the deaf person's ear. This action serves only to bring stares from passers-by and further inhibit the interaction. As described by a deaf lipreader, the approach of the speaker toward the deaf person's ear can also lead to the following:

> At all costs I must keep my line of vision to his face; so I step back. If this is a badly managed encounter we may begin to perform a kind of slow tango. Here is X advancing on my ear, myself retreating step for step, eyes fixed on my partner's face [Wright, 1969: 114].

What occurred is a distancing problem that Hall (1959, 1966) has discussed for cross-cultural encounters.[5]

Americans who meet a non-English speaking foreigner, especially in the states, may cope with that situation in much the same way as hearing people do when they meet a deaf person. Americans may shout, exaggerate their English, or speak English with the "appropriate" accent, whereas hearing people, as noted above, shout, exaggerate their mouth movements, or move closer to the deaf person's ear.

The above incident illustrates another strain that may arise when deaf people attempt to play the hearing role through lipreading. In order to lipread, the deaf person must maintain relatively constant focus on the speaker's face. This constant attention can make hearing speakers uncomfortable because they are rarely used to continual eye contact from the listener (Argyle and Dean, 1965). It may also lead these speakers to shift the position of the face, thus causing the deaf lipreader to miss what was said.

Even if deaf people are successful in lipreading hearing people's spoken words, misunderstandings may still occur. The deaf may lose the information that speech conveys nonverbally—for example, through intonation or emphasis. Consequently, the emotion or intent of the speaker might be misinterpreted (Schiff and Thayer, 1974).

Although lipreading is often inadequate for successfully performing the hearer role, many hearing people commonsensically believe that it is very effective. This belief, which has been historically promoted by educators of the deaf, supports the technique of pretense. Even if the deaf do not understand what is being said, they can pretend to because many hearing people believe that all deaf people can lipread well. To a lesser degree, deaf people may perform the speaker role through substitution of one modality for another. There is no equivalent to lipreading, but performing the speaker *role* requires only appropriate responses which need not always be verbal. As noted before, deaf people who smile and nod their heads in agreement are not only pretending to be hearers but are also giving appropriate responses as speakers. In situations of limited contact, pointing rather than speaking is often appropriate. Deaf people may point to the items on the menu which they wish to order. Who can fault someone for not being able to pronounce some foreign dishes? A few words may accompany the pointing. Though pointing may not be the ordinary response in a restaurant, it often suffices along with other techniques (e.g., collusion, to be discussed next) to maintain the stance than nothing is out of the ordinary.

Substitution is also employed by individuals with other impairments. Blind people who rely on their hearing to tell them when it is safe to cross the street are substituting one sense for another. Often those with impairments are explicitly trained to use their remaining senses and abilities as substitutes for those senses and abilities which are impaired.

In order effectively to substitute one sense or modality of action for another, physically impaired people must be alive to both features of and sensory cues in situations that others take for granted. Thus, the techniques of being alive and of substitution of senses are complementary. The success of each is based on there being *redundant* information in situations. Many different cues, often available through different sensory channels, can inform us of what is happening. The potential problem, of course, is that secondary cues and senses may not always give us as accurate or detailed information about what is occurring as the primary ones do.

Collusion. Other deaf people maintain the hearing's impression that nothing unusual is happening with a little help from their friends. Through collusion with "wise" hearing people, deaf people can often avoid potential communication problems with naive hearing people. That collusion may be intentional and well thought out in advance, or it may be a routine that has slowly, almost subconsciously, developed. Thus in a restaurant, one wise hearing person may order for the entire group of deaf and hearing people. The waitress may be none the wiser. A parallel situation exists when wise foreigners order dinner for their American friends in foreign restaurants. Again, a similar kind of collusion occurs in stigma management when, for example, the blind person's sighted companion guides the blind person through a room (Goffman, 1963).

Collusion is also used by the deaf to perform the speaker role. A hearing friend may do most of the speaking for a deaf person. More subtly, those who have difficulty moderating their speech due to a lack of auditory feedback may arrange for a hearing friend to accompany them and provide visual feedback (e.g., hand signals) in place of the auditory feedback. Backstage work may even take place in order to prepare deaf people for their performances—e.g., hearing friends may coach deaf people in pronunciation or volume. As is the case for training in the substitution of senses, educational programs for the deaf and for those with other impairments are expected to do such backstage work.

Through all four techniques--pretense, being alive, substitution of senses, and collusion—deaf people attempt to maintain the hearing's orientation that nothing unusual is happening and thereby successfully accomplish everyday activities. These four techniques often complement each other or are used in conjunction with one another. They are used by

those with other physical impairments as well as by foreigners.

Managing "Something Unusual is Happening"

In many situations, if not in most, deaf people cannot or
choose not to maintain the impression that nothing is out of
the ordinary. It may be more difficult and less effective to
pretend to be hearing than to let others know of one's
impairment. In these situations, the deaf often explicitly
reveal their impairment and then try to indicate to the
hearing how both can successfully manage the encounter.
Three major strategies are used. Deaf people may implicitly
or explicitly *disclose* that they have an impairment and then
indicate what the hearing should do. Others use a *go-between,* a third party, to pass the messages back and forth.
And some deaf people *manipulate* the hearing's impression of
the type or extent of their impairment in order to facilitate
interaction.

Disclosure. Most of the time, especially when the conversation with the hearing will entail more than a brief exchange, deaf people openly disclose their hearing and speech
limitations to naive hearing people. Other physically disabled
people often do the same. Something is out of the ordinary
which deaf people attempt to guide hearing people through.

Deaf people often attempt to communicate with hearing
people through writing or gestures. While they may be understood, the interaction is rarely smooth and uninhibited. Further, after reading a deaf person's written message and still
relying on the assumption that everyone can hear, hearing
people may speak to rather than write to the deaf person.
When this happens, those deaf who do not lipread must
explicitly state that they have a hearing impairment which
requires the hearing to write rather than speak their message.
Hearing people, though, are often uncomfortable with
writing. They may even leave the deaf person standing with
paper and pencil in hand.

Further, misunderstanding may occur because the writing or gesture of the deaf person is interpreted by the hearing individual within a different symbolic framework from that wherein it was produced (Stokoe and Battison, 1975).

A bank teller given a note asking for a coin bag mistook two deaf mutes for robbers.

"Please give me a zipper bag," read the note that a teenager dressed in white cut-off trousers passed to the teller at the First Federal Savings and Loan Association.

Thinking it was a holdup, the teller triggered an.alarm, police said. The teller then stalled the youth, identified as Robert J. Pokorny, 19, of Painesville, Ohio.

An FBI spokesman said the teenager waited, but after a few moments scribbled another note: I will bring 2,500 coins.

The teller kept stalling, and the youth finally picked up his notes and left with his companion, Howard E. Shuping, 54, of Akron, Ohio.

Witnesses gave police officers and FBI agents a discription of the car, which was traced to a residence in nearby Clearwater.

"The FBI followed Bobby to his grandmother's house," said his aunt, Elsie Pokorny of Clearwater.

"They pulled their guns and told them to stop as they got out of the car, but they couldn't hear it," she said. "I'm thankful they didn't shoot."

Pokorny and Shuping were taken to FBI offices in Tampa, 25 miles away, and detained for questioning. They were released after a Federal attorney said no charges would be filed [The Deaf American, 1973: 29].

While the meaning of the youth's notes seems clear, the bank teller misframed his actions because of the assumption that everyone can hear and speak. The deaf customer did not *explicitly* state that he was deaf, but only ambiguously implied it by writing his request. Therefore, if it is assumed that everyone can hear and speak, then the only reason that people would write a note in a bank is if they were attempting to rob it. Of course, not everyone can hear and speak. Thus, assumptions which are developed in a hearing world can lead to confusion when applied to outsiders in that world.

Go-between. Often deaf people rely on a "wise" hearing person to act as a *go-between* in encounters with naive hearing people. The wise hearing person, often a son or a daughter, will translate the remarks of the naive hearing person in sign language. If the deaf person does not speak intelligibly, the go-between will translate the sign language into spoken language. The parallel to encounters between foreigners is obvious. This technique often works reasonably well, but a few problems may arise.

If the go-between is unsophisticated in the matter being discussed, then satisfactorily conveying the information to both sides may be difficult. Such could be the case if the go-between for a deaf couple is their young hearing child. The same problem may occur when first-generation immigrant children interpret for their immigrant parents. These examples suggest a related problem. Personal matters (e.g., illnesses or financial dealings) are often embarrassing to discuss through a third party—particularly a third party who is a young, unsophisticated child.

The role of the go-between may also expand beyond what the impaired person intended. Normals may direct more of their attention to the go-between than either the impaired person or the go-between feels is necessary. Thus, waitresses may ask sighted companions of blind people what the latter wish to order (Gowman, 1956). On the other hand, the go-between may gradually monopolize the interaction. Rather than interpret what is said, the go-between makes decisions for the impaired person or the foreigner. As I noted in Chapters 2 and 3, deaf people often complain of not being fully informed when a go-between handles a telephone conversation for them. They become the third party.

Manipulation. Other deaf people may acknowledge that something unusual is happening, but manipulate the impression that hearing people have of what, exactly, is occurring. Goffman (1963: 94) argues that those pass may present signs of their failing as signs of another attribute which is less stigmatized. The deaf may use similar techniques, but not in order to manage their putatively spoiled identities. In fact, the deaf may present themselves as *more* impaired than they are in order to manage the encounter. The manipulations, though, fit the assumptions that the hearing bring to the encounters.

For example, those deaf individuals whose speech may lead hearing people mistakenly to identify them as hearing, sometimes use a simple strategy. In those situations where prolonged contact will not occur, the deaf may write their message rather than speak it. The deaf man who had problems at ticket counters does so now when requesting airline information (Jacobs, 1974). The deaf man not only avows his deviance of deafness (Turner, 1972), but implies a second discrediting trait of mutism which he does not possess. The strategy, though, allows the deaf person to complete the interaction successfully. The blind may use a similar strategy:

One totally blind boy who had a very normal appearance suffered so many unfortunate experiences from being taken for sighted that he began to carry a cane even though he made not the slightest use of it in getting about his environment [Lemert, 1951: 109-110].

Different strategies are used by those deaf whose speech becomes unintelligible to hearing people once hearing people know of the deafness. Some deaf people keep their impairment a secret from the hearing person. Others will reveal it as soon as they feel the hearing listener has become accustomed to their speech. Some use manipulation. They wear a hearing aid (Jacobs, 1974). Though the deaf person's speech does not improve, it remains intelligible to the hearing person because the deaf person is no longer viewed as a grossly defective hearer. The deaf person is only mildly defective (i.e., "hard of hearing") and still capable of speaking intelligibly. In passing as hard of hearing, these deaf people are not concerned with their spoiled identities. Rather, they are using a practical, learned strategy of manipulation which allows the interaction with the hearing person to proceed more smoothly.

As noted before, though, hearing people may treat deaf people as hard of hearing. The hearing shout or move closer to deaf people's ears (Webb et al., 1966: 150). Deaf people who wear a hearing aid so that their speech will remain intelligible to hearing people may find that it becomes even more difficult to lipread a hearing person as the latter shouts or advances toward their ears. A strategy to combat one strain may increase the likelihood of another.

DISCUSSION

Unlike many other outsiders, the deaf are physically disabled. Their impairment and its accompanying limitations may profoundly disrupt interaction with the hearing. The same is true for other physically disabled outsiders. Consequently, stigmatization cannot fully explain the often awkward encounters between the deaf and the hearing.

Several factors seem to account for this overemphasis on stigmatization. Labeling theorists have often investigated or emphasized the visibly disabled (Davis, 1961; Barry 1973; Levitin, 1975). Therefore, the disabled's "differentness" was often apparent to both the nondisabled as well as to the sociologist. Further, much of the research has focused on the physically disabled who acquired their impairments later in life. Often they had not resolved issues of personal and social acceptance (Ladieu et al., 1948). While those born impaired or who have been impaired for a long time may continue to cope with stigmatization, that issue may not be paramount in their lives. As I explained in the previous chapter, members of the deaf community often deal with particular stigmatizing behaviors of the hearing by ignoring them. For example, members are so used to the stares that their signing attracts that they no longer pay attention to them. While members are ambivalent about their deafness, they derive a sense of belonging and wholeness from their fellow members of the deaf community. Consequently, the lack of social acceptance among members of the hearing world becomes less important, because acceptance is found within the deaf community. I suspect that much the same could be said for those who are members of other communities of outsiders. Finally, as in much previous thinking on outsiders in general (Goode, 1978), researchers have often assumed, even while denying it, that the physically disableds' lives are radically different from the nondisableds'. If that is so, then what problems they face and how they cope with them must be different too (Carroll, 1961).

CONCLUSION

An important task that the deaf face, as well as everyone else, whether they are outsiders or not, is to accomplish everyday activities competently. In trying to do so, the deaf often experience awkward, embarrassing, and unsatisfactory encounters with the hearing. Consequently, while the deaf cannot avoid the hearing world, they often seek out those with whom easy communication is possible—other deaf people. Awkward encounters with the hearing are part of the experiences which members of the deaf community share with one another. Those experiences reinforce the members' identification and participation with one another. Although the deaf community is not merely a response to the deaf's frustrating interaction with the hearing, it certainly does provide the social setting within which relaxed, uninhibited communication for the deaf typically takes place.

NOTES

1. The accompanying limitations of deafness (e.g., unintelligible speech or inability to control the volume of one's speech) are more likely to occur for those who were born deaf or became deaf at an early age. Those who lost their hearing later in life would not experience the full range of strains and misunderstandings that I discuss. Of course, the latter would not be members of deaf communities.

2. Such assumptions may lead to amusing incidents. For example, a deaf chemist who works for a consulting firm was called by a client one day. Clients send the firm samples to analyze and problems to solve. The client telephoned the firm and told the operator that he wished to speak with Mr. Harris about a report that the chemist had written for him. The operator told the man that he could not talk with Mr. Harris because Mr. Harris cannot talk over the phone. He is deaf. The client replied that that was alright; please have Mr. Harris call him back later.

3. One deaf respondent explained that during World War II he and other deaf men who had good speech were drafted and inducted into the army. The induction officers, already wary, did not believe that these men were deaf. They talked so well. Once in the army, they were discovered to be deaf and excused from duty.

4. A similar term, "blindism," denotes the self-stimulating body movements of the blind due to the lack of visual feedback and stimulation. The blind manipulate their faces, tilt their bodies, and have tics and twitches of the face which disrupt communication with the sighted (Carroll, 1961).

5. Some initial research (Moyer, 1975) suggests that hearing-impaired students who are strangers stand further apart during a signed conversation than do hearing students who are strangers during a voice conversation. The implications for deaf-hearing encounters need to be explored.

Conclusion

Throughout this book I have examined several major aspects of the lives of outsiders in a hearing world. Chapter 2 examined the community of deaf people. Chapters 3 and 4 explored various facets of the identity and self-perceptions of members of the deaf community. Chapters 5 and 6 discussed the everyday interaction between the deaf and the hearing from two different perspectives. The deaf community, the identity of its members and the interaction between the deaf and the hearing are interrelated. Each can only be fully understood in relation to the others. The interrelationships of these three aspects of deaf people's lives were often only implied in the preceding chapters. In the following pages I make those relationships explicit.

There is a second interrelationship which I want to make explicit in these concluding pages. That is the interrelationship between being deaf and being hearing and, more generally, between being an outsider and being a member of the larger social world. The identities and social realities of each group, depend on the other's. It makes no sense to speak of a *deaf* community or of the identity of *deaf* people without there being a hearing world. Conversely, what it means to be a *hearing* person can only be fully understood within the context of the historical and present relationship between hearing and deaf people. What it means to be hearing does not just involve the ability to hear. It also includes assumptions that hearing people make about themselves and the deaf—advantages which hearing people enjoy or think that they enjoy because of their abilities, as well as advantages which they create for themselves (to the disadvantage of the deaf); the heavy emphasis on speaking and lipreading; the fears of losing one's hearing and so on. Therefore, while those who create and control the larger social world and those who are outsiders in that world are in conflict, in a fundamental sense, each cannot do without the other.

COMMUNITY, IDENTITY, AND INTERACTION

Membership in the deaf community is achieved through identification with the deaf, shared experiences of being hearing impaired and participation in the community's activities. Those shared experiences of being hearing impaired involve the problems of navigating in a hearing world. The often unsatisfying interaction is due both to the hearing's stigmatization of the deaf and to the inhibited and awkward communication between the deaf and the hearing. As children and as adults, the members of the deaf community experience frustration and embarrassment when navigating in a hearing world. However, within the deaf community, easy and "natural" communication is usually taken for granted. In the hearing world it is rarely achieved. Within the deaf community there is no shame in being deaf. Within the hearing world the deaf were often made to feel ashamed until they grew more accustomed to the shaming behavior of the hearing. The deaf community is, then, partially a response to the unsatisfying interaction which the deaf experience in a hearing world. The community provides a sanctuary from the curiosity, ridicule, and awkward communication which the deaf often encounter among the hearing.

While membership in the deaf community is based on identification with the deaf, membership in the community supports and strengthens deaf people's identity and adjustment to deafness. A sense of wholeness and belonging is achieved within the deaf community which is lacking within the hearing world. Because life within the community is fulfilling, there is rarely any overwhelming desire to hear. I suspect that deaf people who are not members would be more concerned about their hearing losses than those who are. However, members live within a hearing world where deafness is a drawback. Therefore, for very practical reasons, members would enjoy being able to hear again. It would help them navigate better in a hearing world. As members, though, they embrace their deafness. This is why sign language is an integral feature for most members' identities. At the same time, though, members cannot easily forget the desires of their hearing parents and teachers for them to become like hearing people; speech therefore takes on some significance within the deaf community. As are other outsiders, the deaf are ambivalent about what makes them outsiders.

Membership in the deaf community and identification with the deaf influence the interaction of the deaf in a hearing world. It influences their stigmatization. Members of the community, though certainly not all deaf people (Warfield, 1948), have little desire to pass as hearing. Managing their putative stigmata is of relatively little importance to them. Further, signing is an integral part of the deaf community and of its members' identities. It is also the most effective means of communication among the members of the community. Consequently, members are likely to sign to one another in public even if their hearing children or hearing parents are ashamed of doing so. Signing identifies members as deaf and sets them up for stigmatizing behavior from the hearing. However, the stares, ridicule and attempts of the hearing to suppress or change signing only redoubles the importance of signing to the deaf community. This, in turn, helps to create and maintain the conflict between signers and speakers within the deaf community. Signers perceive speakers to be not as fully committed to the deaf world as they should be.

Membership in the deaf community may lead to additional, future strain when the deaf encounter the hearing. Membership may decrease hearing-impaired people's desire to improve their speech and lipreading abilities. From a sense of belonging within the deaf community comes less of a desire to be like hearing people, which means to be able to hear and speak. Certainly, many members do not use hearing aids who, from the hearing world's point of view, could benefit from them. Others may have resisted learning to speak or do not use their speech with hearing people out of resentment of their parents' and teachers' heavy emphasis on oralism. Other members have been ridiculed for their odd-sounding speech. Therefore, they may not speak, even though their speech is understandable. In either case, navigation in the hearing world becomes more difficult. And as I noted in Chapter 5, the strained and inhibited communication between the deaf and the hearing makes it less likely that the stigmatization and stereotyping of the deaf will appreciably decrease.

If, within their community, the deaf can partially ignore the hearing, the situation changes in the world of work. There the deaf are dependent on the hearing for jobs. Consequently, they are concerned about the image which the hearing hold of them. Therefore, peddling, which spoils their image and thereby jeopardizes their employment opportunities, is deviant within the deaf community.

The deaf community, the identity of its members, and the interaction with the hearing are interrelated. Difficulties which arise in one area may be solved in another, though solutions themselves may give rise to additional difficulties. For example, members of the deaf community try to "solve" their identity and adjustment problems by affirming that they are deaf and embracing sign language. Commitment to sign language, though, may increase difficulties for the deaf when they navigate in a hearing world. To understand fully these three aspects of deaf people's lives, we need to view them in relation to one another.

The deaf are only one group among many who are outsiders. By recognizing that, we better appreciate the processes of society which create and maintain outsiders, whether they be deaf or not. Individuals do create reality. Some, though, are more powerful than others. They monopolize reality. They define for themselves and others what skills, abilities, and characteristics are needed to be "normal" in society. Some of those attributes seem "obviously" unjust and unnecessary, though they may have been taken for granted in the past. Being white is an outstanding example.

Other attributes and skills seem clearly important. Requiring them for various activities appears just. Disabilities or the inability to read, write, or speak English are viewed as objective limitations. We assume that if people are disabled or do not know English, then those people should expect to be excluded from certain activities and opportunities and to face greater difficulties than they would if they were "normal." That seems reasonable. However, when you think about it, how reasonable is it to require that computer operators be able to hear? On the basis of that requirement, deaf people have been denied jobs as computer operators in the federal government (Bowe et al., 1973). Or how relevant is height to being a police officer? The Boston police department has already accepted a five-foot, one-inch woman, which has caused no problems; but it refuses to accept a four-foot, three-inch man who passed the entrance exam and the marksmanship and physical tests (Newsweek, 1979). However, it is specifically those assumptions made by the monopolizers of reality which create and maintain people as outsiders that are in need of the most thorough examinations.

Deafness, as well as other disabilities, seem to be objective limitations. Those present limitations might be far less, though, if particular assumptions about the deaf were examined. Throughout this book I have explored assumptions and routine practices of the hearing which increase the limitations of deafness beyond those caused by the impairment. In Chapter 6 I analyzed several assumptions and behaviors of hearing people that increase communication difficulty that starts with deafness. In Chapter 5 I discussed the ideas of master status and spread, which further limit deaf people. In Chapters 2 and 3 I examined the desire of educators to suppress or change sign language so that deaf people would better fit into a hearing world. Yet, deaf people's entrance into that world is difficult, as we saw in Chapters 5 and 6. In Chapter 4 I noted how peddling plays on the sympathy of hearing people. Yet that sympathy again limits deaf people, for it is extended to the deaf because they are seen as having few skills. Specific assumptions and practices like these need to be examined. After critically examining such assumptions, we may decide, for example, that not only should deaf adults be an integral feature of the education of deaf children, but perhaps many could play an important role in the education of hearing children as well (Merrill, 1979). The creation of new approaches, in turn, requires us to be critical of what we have accepted for so long.

INTERDEPENDENCE BETWEEN
THE DEAF AND THE HEARING

The deaf community, the identity of its members, and their interaction with the hearing world are interrelated. The previous chapters often only implicitly stated such relationships. The past several pages have made those interdependencies explicit. In a similar way, the social realities of being deaf and being hearing are interdependent.

Being an outsider is meaningful in relationship to and primarily in contrast with those who monopolize reality. Being an outsider is only possible if there are those who are not outsiders. Being black has meaning only if there are white people. Blindness must be contrasted to sight in order to be fully understood. Homosexuality takes on its importance within a heterosexual world, and so on. Through the larger social world's oppression of outsiders and through outsiders' efforts to cope with that oppression develops the distinctiveness of being an outsider. As Robert Blauner (1972:

140-141) observed of the paradoxical debt that black culture
owes to oppression, racism is the

> single most important source of the developing ethnic people-
> hood. Racism has been such an omnipresent reality that the
> direct and indirect struggle against it makes up the core of black
> history in America.

Deaf people can only be understood in relationship to
their position in a hearing world. To view them outside of
that context is fundamentally to distort their experiences. In
the preceding chapters I have explored the lives of deaf
people *within* a hearing world. The deaf community is partially a response to the deaf's unsatisfying interaction in a
hearing world. It is an outgrowth of shared experiences in
childhood and adolescence and in educational programs for
the deaf. It is an affirmation of being deaf in a world where
hearing is taken for granted. The structure of the deaf community, particularly the distinction between signers and
speakers, can only be understood as a response of deaf people
to hearing educators' and parents' emphasis on becoming as
much like hearing people as possible. The ambivalence of
members of the deaf community about their deafness is due
to members being caught between their community (and
their affirmation of their deafness) and the hearing world.
Peddling is deviant within the deaf community because members perceive it as spoiling their image and thereby also
jeopardizing their chances to be rightfully included in activities controlled by the hearing world. Peddling is seen as
supporting the historically subjugated position of the deaf.
The deaf are stigmatized by the hearing and awkward, and
often unsatisfying experiences arise when the deaf encounter
the hearing. Deaf people can be outsiders *only* in a hearing
world.

Equally important, though, is that *not* being an outsider--
being an insider, being a monopolizer of reality—is only
completely meaningful in relation to those who are outsiders.
How could being white have any significance if it were not

contrasted with the position of those who are not white? How could the moral uprightness of many heterosexuals make sense if they did not contrast themselves to the presumed moral depravity of homosexuals? There is a fundamental interdependence between those who create and control the larger social world and those who are outsiders in that world. Or as Everett Hughes (1964: 31) put it, "an in-group is one only because there are out-groups." Yet, this fundamental point is often overlooked. The thoughts, feelings, and practices of those who monopolize reality are rarely considered problematic. The relationship between them and outsiders is taken for granted. That is the way the world naturally should be. It is only in moments of pity or revulsion, and then only fleetingly, that a few of those who create and control the larger social world glimpse the fact that their identities are tied to those who are outsiders in that world.

In developing a sense of who we are, we compare ourselves to some people and contrast ourselves to others. We use both similarities and differences in establishing our identities. Similarities enable us to establish ties to one another, to recognize common concerns that we share with others, to recognize a unity of purpose and being.

Through contrasts, though, we assert our distinctiveness or at least what we perceive to be our distinctiveness. Through opposition to others we proclaim our unique identities. In declaring who we are *not* like, we affirm what we are like. We often draw the sharpest distinctions between ourselves and other people whom third parties would see as quite similar. A politician claims not to be like those other self-serving legislators. A homosexual abhors the "swishy" and effeminate gay. The deaf signer questions the commitment of the deaf speaker. Without contrasts, many of the categories that we use in identifying ourselves make little sense. The notion of what it is to be a male takes on significance only in contrast to being a female. To be religious has its fullest meaning only in relation to those who are not religious. If all were wise, then there would be no such thing as wisdom. As Irving Tallman (1976: 96) clearly states:

Who we are is established according to criteria which identify us with one group and differentiate us from others. Thus our identity depends on similarities to some people; dissimilarities to others. The identity of a policeman, for example, requires the existence of nonpoliceman, just as the identity of an honest man requires the existence of those who are dishonest.

Identities, though, are not neutral. We *evaluate* ourselves as well as others. We praise some characteristics and behaviors and condemn others. We decide that we as well as others are more or less worthy people. Contrasts play a role in this drama. To the extent that we are concerned with our own worth, we are also concerned with the worth of those whom we contrast ourselves to. We gain in worth to the extent that others lose, and vice versa (Douglas, 1970). By downgrading others, we upgrade our own selves in contrast. By upgrading ourselves, we downgrade others.

Individuals not only engage in this process of evaluation, but so do groups and nations. For example, in characterizing certain ethnic groups as stupid, nowadays most noticeably Polish people, Americans support their own national sense of self-worth (Greenfield, 1979). Disparaging jokes about Polish people redound to the benefit of those who are not Polish. Over the years, other nationalities have served a similar purpose for Americans.

Perhaps the most important evaluations we make of ourselves are moral ones. We are forever deciding who and what is good or evil, moral or immoral, respectable or deviant. How do we recognize who or what is good, moral or respectable? We recognize them because they are *not* evil, immoral, or deviant. These basic moral categories with which we evaluate ourselves and others are interdependent. In Western society at least, they do not seem to be able to exist without the other (Douglas, 1970). Through establishing categories of evil, immorality, and deviance, and then contrasting ourselves with people whom we place into those categories, we assert both our own identities and distinctiveness, and our moral worth and superiority. As Kai Erikson (1964: 15) notes, deviants inform us of "what shapes the devil can assume," and in doing so, they show us "the difference between the inside of the group and the outside." Evil, immorality, and deviance are a necessary part of society. Without them we could not recognize good, morality, and respectability. Therefore, even if we "eradicate our present evils, we will simply construct new ones" (Douglas, 1970: 5). According to Durkheim (1966), if we do away with crime then we will elevate what used to be considered trivial offenses to the level of serious crimes. Although they may change their form, notions of evil, immorality, and deviance will always be created and maintained. In contrast to them we know what is good and are able to support our own moral worth. Outsiders serve much the same purpose.

Outsiders serve as a "*foil* to ideals of health and the good" (Adam, 1978: 42). According to Adam (1978: 50), while the specifics of each portrait may vary, the composite portrait of Jews, blacks, and gays serves to "convince the majority of its identity as the 'good.' " By putting and keeping people in subordinate positions, by making them outsiders, those who monopolize reality assure themselves that, in contrast to outsiders, they are morally superior people. They may also assure themselves of cheap labor, convenient scapegoats, and so on. If outsiders did not exist, then they would be created.

The deaf and others who are disabled serve as a foil for the nondisabled in society. By portraying the disabled as different, odd, or not quite normal and by routinely putting them in an inferior position, the nondisabled assert their moral superiority. The nondisabled also expect the disabled to agree. They expect the disabled to mourn their losses. Thus, blindness and the rehabilitation of the blind are viewed in terms of death and rebirth (Carroll, 1961). Mourning is a sign that those losses are indeed important. If the disabled do not mourn their losses, then they threaten the security and superiority of the nondisabled, which are partly based on the fact that they, at least, have not suffered such losses (Wright, 1960).

The nondisabled also expect the disabled eagerly to jump at the chance for salvation which the nondisabled offer. That road to salvation is simple: Become as much as possible like the nondisabled. By offering this chance for salvation, the nondisabled reinforce their identity as good and their feelings of superiority in two ways. They demonstrate their concern and generosity for those less fortunate than they. They also reassure themselves that the characteristics upon which they base their superiority are important ones. What better flattery is there than imitation, even if it is at the suggestion or even the command of those who are flattered?

In this light, the overwhelming emphasis of hearing educators on the training of speech and lipreading skills for the deaf, and their rejection of sign language takes on additional significance. In a similar manner Americans have believed in teaching foreigners " 'democracy,' modern technology, and other aspects of 'our way of life,' " (Dexter, 1964: 41). Middle-class folks have urged the poor to adopt middle-class values (Valentine, 1968). And many whites seem to have the most respect for those blacks whom many other blacks would call Uncle Toms.

When outsiders reject those ways to salvation, though, those who monopolize reality feel betrayed. Thus, Americans find it hard to tolerate the fact that foreigners wish to remain "*fundamentally* alien" (Dexter, 1964: 41). Many whites cannot understand why blacks may not only want to retain but actively promote separate schools, organizations, traditions, and so on, when given the chance to do otherwise. However, if outsiders jumped at those chances for salvation, then they would be damning their identities and realities, which have personally developed over years and have collectively developed over centuries of struggle with the larger social world.

So it is for hearing people and for outsiders in a hearing world. In the past, many hearing educators simply resigned themselves to the fact that once deaf youth left school many became signers and joined the deaf community. The effort continues, though. While oralism has given way to total communication, mainstreaming is now becoming the way to salvation.

Mainstreaming is a recent term in special education, though the philosophy which embodies it has slowly developed over decades. It asserts that children with special education needs, whether those needs are due to physical disabilities, emotional problems, learning difficulties, or whatever, should be mainstreamed or integrated into regular classrooms as much as possible. Of course, additional training of teachers as well as support services would theoretically be provided. Integration in the classroom would not only provide better education for the child with special needs, but would lead to greater integration later in life. Proponents of mainstreaming argue that children with special needs too often are segregated in special institutions and programs without thorough examination of the basis for that segregation. Many receive no education at all. Segregation in education is likely to lead to segregation when the children become adults. Through court decisions and federal law (PL 94-142, the Education for All Handicapped Children Act of 1975) mainstreaming has become an important, but complex and controversial, issue in education on (Birch, 1974; Jones, 1976; Reynolds, 1977; Special Learing Corporation, 1978). Notice how this position echoes Alexander Graham Bell's criticism, almost 100 years ago, of the education of the deaf (Chapter 2).

While positive benefits may result from mainstreaming, some deaf and "wise" hearing professionals are leary of it as applied to deaf children. Some are concerned that mainstreaming may lead to the placement of deaf children in regular classrooms wherein the appropriate services (e.g., interpreters) are not provided to meet the children's needs (Brill, 1975). Others argue that deaf children need the social, recreational, and interpersonal activities that only separate programs, preferably residential programs, can provide. These professionals are concerned that mainstreaming may interfere with the deaf child's development of an identity as a deaf person. As Vernon and Estes (1975: 4) note:

Integrated [educational] programs also have a tendency to take from the deaf youth the feeling of closeness to other deaf people that can be so valuable.

Mainstreaming of deaf children in classes for the hearing and later as adults in the hearing world is unlikely to be completely successful because of communication difficulties.[1] Nevertheless, some deaf and "wise" hearing people have recognized it as a threat to the deaf community. Consequently, it is viewed with caution. In maintaining their own identities, the deaf and other outsiders help maintain the distinction and contrast between themselves and the larger social world. Ironically, while those who create and control the larger social world and those who are outsiders in that world are in conflict with one another, their identities and existence are inextricably bound together.

However, the relationship between those who create and control the social world and outsiders in that world is never fixed. It is always changing, if only slowly. In the past decade, important changes have occurred for the deaf. Total communication has become the predominant mode of communication in classes for deaf students. Through state and federal law, interpreting for the deaf is out of the closet and into legal, medical, and other settings. Deaf awareness and deaf pride are no longer merely slogans. Television programs about the deaf or with deaf characters are appearing more frequently. Captioning of television programs so that hearing-impaired viewers can fully enjoy them will soon be provided on a regular basis nationwide. Presently it exists on a limited scale. An increasing number of television news programs include a sign language interpreter. Deaf individuals are gaining administrative positions in educational programs for the deaf. In the same way that the 1960s was the civil rights era for black Americans, the 1970s has been the civil rights era for disabled Americans. The deaf and other disabled groups have successfully lobbied for the enactment and implementation of legislation to help end discrimination against them.

The Rehabilitation Act of 1973 and its implementation through federal regulations of the past several years is the most far-reaching manifestation of this legislation. Times are indeed changing.

We should be cautious, however, as we view the future of the deaf. The history of other outsiders warns us that centuries of oppression and neglect will not be righted in a few years. For example, the turmoil which surrounds school busing is a dramatic indication that school desegregation has yet to be achieved, even though the Supreme Court's landmark ruling was more than twenty-five years ago. Presently, gays throughout America struggle to protect rights which they have won against moral crusades to repeal gay-rights legislation. Even as the deaf and other disabled groups take pride in their efforts which resulted in recent legislation to end discrimination against them, they are also aware that it took several years, plus many demonstrations and marches, for regulations to be written which implemented that legislation. It will probably be up to the courts in the decade ahead to interpret the legislation and regulations, as it has been in the case of black Americans. And as in the case of black Americans, the court rulings are likely to be mixed.[2] In fact, this has already proven to be the case. Therefore, with an optimism tempered by the history of other outsider groups, I look forward to the future of those who are outsiders in a hearing world.

NOTES

1. From personal experience (my wife's), mainstreaming is most successful when hearing children learn to sign. In these cases, deaf children are not isolated within the hearing classroom (even though they have an interpreter), but, rather, become a part of the class. Both deaf and hearing children adjust in these successful situations of mainstreaming. Such mutual adjustments within the hearing world, though, are much more difficult.

2. See *In the Mainstream*, a newsletter published by Mainstream, Incorporated, for a continuing account of court rulings which affect the disabled.

Research Appendix

As I mentioned in the Introduction, my parents are deaf, my wife teaches deaf children, and I taught at a state school for the deaf for one year before beginning graduate work in sociology. My experiences have had a profound impact on this book: They have influenced the topic I chose to pursue, outsiders in a hearing world, as well as the perspective from which I view that topic, the perspective of deaf people. My personal experiences have also aided me in doing the research itself. When investigating a social scene, several research problems must be solved. Among those are gaining access to the people whom you are interested in understanding and then developing and maintaining their trust. My experience has helped me deal with both of these issues.

ACCESS

The deaf are outsiders in a hearing world. Yet, to the deaf, the hearing are also outsiders. As I discussed in Chapter 2, the members of the deaf community often mistrust hearing people. Based on their personal experiences, members are suspicious of the intentions of the hearing. The same holds true for outsiders in general. They often reject those who reject them. Gays do not generally welcome straights into their social world. Blacks are wary of whites. Being the son of deaf parents, though, has helped me gain access to the deaf community in two specific ways.

183

First, even though my parents live on the East Coast, several people whom I interviewed knew them and therefore were happy to talk with me. A few even knew of me. Thus, I relied on the personal relations that my parents had with deaf people in the Chicago area to "get my foot in the door." Through a snowballing technique (to be discussed later), these deaf individuals referred me to others who, in turn, referred me to still others. In this way I was led to people who had no idea who my parents were. However, once they found out that my parents were deaf and that I had been referred to them by a friend or an acquaintance, I was welcomed into their lives. At a club for the deaf, some of its members approached me because they recognized my name. Having deaf parents helped me get initial contacts in the deaf community. Just as in the everyday world where who you know can make a difference, personal contacts can help sociologists in their research.

My personal experiences also gave me access to the language of the deaf people whom I interviewed. My respondents communicated in various ways. Some spoke reasonably well. They could be understood by naive hearing people. Others' speech would be intelligible only to those who are familiar with the deaf. Many did not speak. Some lipread and others used their residual hearing when listening to speakers. The majority of the members of the deaf community are most comfortable signing. For many it is their native language. Without knowing sign language, researchers of the deaf community would face many of the same difficulties that deaf people do in navigating through a hearing world. As do the deaf, the researcher could rely on paper and pencil or an interpreter. But neither approach is entirely satisfactory, as I discussed in Chapter 6. Each approach puts additional distance between the researcher and the deaf men and women. Here again, my background aided my research.

Although sign language is not my native language, I am relatively fluent in it. Several deaf people thought that I was deaf until I explained to them that I was hearing, but had learned to sign from my parents who are deaf. At times, though, I did not understand what the deaf respondents were signing. In most cases, my asking the deaf individuals to repeat their messages cleared up my lack of understanding. A few times, though, I still did not understand even after the third or so repetition. In these cases, which concerned minor points, I simply nodded my head and the conversation proceeded. The deaf may do much the same thing, as I noted in Chapter 6. Rather than jeopardize the remainder of my interview with these individuals, I simply let the point pass. Again, having deaf parents allowed me access not only to particular deaf people, but also to their language.

TRUST

Developing and maintaining trust with the people whom one is trying to understand is a crucial issue. It is particularly crucial when one is investigating a group of outsiders, whether they be deaf, black, gay, or whatever. By the very nature of the historical and social relation between outsiders and the larger world, one would expect outsiders not to trust intruders from that wider world, even if those intruders are well-meaning researchers. Without developing the trust and confidence of those who are interviewed, researchers cannot be sure if they can rely on what they are being told. An elaborate game of impression mangement may be taking place (Goffman, 1959). The outsiders give the intruder from the larger world what the latter already expects to hear. A black folk song makes exactly that point when it states that blacks have one mind for white people to see and another mind which is really theirs (Ames, 1950). The same situation could happen when the intruder into the deaf community is hearing.

For example, in studying the deaf community in the Washington, D.C. metropolitan area, Jerome Schein (1968) found that deaf interviewers were superior to their hearing counterparts in obtaining information from deaf respondents. Deaf interviewers had a lower refusal rate than did hearing interviewers. They were also more likely than hearing interviewers to make a positive impression on the deaf respondent such that the respondent would be willing to be interviewed again. These findings suggest that a hearing interviewer might obtain distorted information from a deaf respondent.

If there is distortion, what would it be like? There has been no research regarding the possible bias in studies of the deaf by hearing interviewers. However, studies on bias in research involving black respondents and white interviewers can suggest what distortions may occur when deaf individuals are interviewed by hearing researchers.

Research on the effects of white interviewers on black individuals' responses indicates that blacks distort their answers so as to present a more idyllic picture of their feelings to whites than to blacks (Phillips, 1971). Jerome Sattler (1970: 151), after reviewing ten studies, concluded that

findings from most studies indicate that white interviewers usually elicited more docile and subservient replies from Negro
respondents than did the Negro interviewers.

Thomas Pettigrew (1964: 50-51) found that blacks showed less
militance and fewer feelings of victimization to white interviewers than
to the black interviewers. For example, 87% of the blacks interviewed
by blacks in a Boston study agreed that the "trouble with most white
people is that they think they are better than other people." Only 66%
of the blacks interviewed by whites agreed with that statement.

Blacks tend to be more conservative and show less outrage to whites
than to blacks. This distortion in blacks' answers to white interviewers
seems to occur particularly over sensitive issues which affect black-
white relationships (Williams, 1964). Thus, a question dealing with
sit-ins is more likely to produce distortion than one dealing with
favorite car models. The key issue in this distortion seems to be the
mistrust that blacks have of whites (which may be well founded) and
the lack of empathy which blacks feel whites have for them. The white
skin color is a signal to blacks to beware. This research concerning
another group of outsiders, black Americans, suggests that the information a hearing researcher would obtain from the deaf would be more
idyllic and less militant than what a deaf researcher might obtain. A
hearing researcher might miss some of the outrage felt by the deaf,
especially with respect to their relations with the hearing. Thus, a
"conservative" bias may exist in the results of hearing researchers who
investigate the deaf community. Two well-known men in the deaf
community, whom I first contacted in order to get the names and
addresses of other deaf people, warned me that I might face resistance
from many deaf people. The two were not sure that deaf people would
"open up" to a hearing person.

Again, my background aided me in establishing trust with the
members of the deaf community who shared their lives with me.
Through first contacting people who knew my parents, and then
contacting those whom I was referred to, I was able to build on the
personal relationships that deaf people had with one another and which
I indirectly was a part of. This snowballing technique, which began with
the personal relations that my parents had with other deaf people, no
doubt helped me minimize refusals. A low refusal rate is one small
indication that trust has been established.

Only five people refused to be interviewed. Two of these had never
answered their letters, and it is possible that the letters had not been

delivered. A third refused, saying that he and his wife did not have enough time for the interview. A deaf woman agreed to an interview, but later declined. Another woman, who also agreed to an interview, was forced to refuse because her husband felt that nothing would be served by it. The deaf man noted, quite correctly, that in the past there has been a great deal of talk about improving conditions for the deaf, but relatively little had been done. Another interview, he felt, would make little difference. The wife was willing, and it would have been easy to approach her another time when her husband was not at home. I chose not to, though, because I did not think it was appropriate to do so.

A low refusal rate is only one indication that trust has been established. There are other signs as well. A hearing woman of deaf parents told me that her husband was concerned that I was interviewing her while she was alone. The woman told her husband that because I had deaf parents (even though she did not know them personally) everything would be alright.

Because of my background, I was interested in understanding rather than judging my deaf respondents. This became clear to those who shared their lives with me. I was a "wise" hearing person who would not stigmatize the deaf as do the hearing. The King of the Peddlers, discussed in Chapter 4, granted me an interview even though his hearing son was reluctant. During the interview, the peddler remarked to a deaf friend who walked into his office that I was alright. I was alright because I was willing to listen and was interested in understanding his life and business rather than criticizing him. He not only answered my questions but showed me his club room, where he held private parties. On the walls of the room were hundreds of pictures of former employees, as well as newspaper clippings concerning his business. He even proudly showed me his receipt for a check for several tens of thousands of dollars which he had paid to the Internal Revenue Service for back taxes he owed. With other respondents I ate dinner or shared a snack. I was welcomed back for additional interviews by each person that I asked. These are small but specific indications that trust was established between myself and the deaf men and women whom I interviewed.

Nevertheless, the reader must be aware of the possible "conservative" bias in the preceding chapters. For example, in Chapter 3 I argued that members of the deaf community are ambivalent about their deafness. They have both positive and negative feelings about it. One might argue, however, that members really do feel a tragic sense of loss and anger about themselves and their hearing impairment, but that they will not display those feelings to a hearing person. That distortion is possible, though I think minimal in this case, if one considers the candor with which the respondents talked about other sensitive issues, such as relationships among themselves and with the hearing.

My personal experiences had a profound impact on this book. Those experiences influenced the topic selected and the perspective I pursued, as well as aided me in doing the research itself. A discussion of the impact of my personal experiences on this book, though, does not fully describe the research process.

GATHERING DATA

In the summer of 1975, I approached two well-known deaf men in the Chicago area and explained my interests to them. From them I obtained the names of several deaf and "hard of hearing" individuals whom they felt would be helpful to me. By telephone, letter, TTY, or personal appearance, I contacted many, though not all, of those people that the two deaf men had mentioned. From those whom I contacted, I obtained the names of friends and acquaintances who might be interesting to talk with for one reason or another (for example, the man mentioned in Chapter 2 who regained much of his hearing, but still remained involved in the deaf community.) I also obtained the names of hearing people who were counselors or ministers to the deaf or in some way familiar with deaf people. From those additional people I obtained new names, and from the latter I obtained even more.

This snowballing technique allowed me to generate contacts with a wide variety of deaf people who varied by age, education, and communication preference and skill (which are important dimensions in the deaf community, as I examined in Chapter 2). This technique would not enable me to uncover deaf individuals who are unknown to the deaf community. This would be a serious limitation had I been interested in analyzing the deaf population. Members of the deaf community, though, were my focus. Yet I felt that I was overlooking what educators call the low verbal deaf, those deaf people, whether they finished school or not, who have very limited ability with English and usually a low skilled job as a result. I asked a key informant to provide me with the names of such people, and I was soon interviewing again.

Contacting the deaf people was not always easy. Many did have telephones, and though they may not have been able to use them, their children could relay my message to them. Others had no phones. Some had TTYs. I did not have one, but several times I used the TTYs of people whom I interviewed or of a university which trained teachers of the deaf. To some I wrote letters, with others I made a personal appearance in order to set up an interview for a later time. The problems that I encountered in contacting the deaf—delays, inability to change appointments, and difficulty in reaching them (part of the methodology that is rarely discussed in textbooks)—reflect similar features of interaction among the deaf. How are the deaf to contact one another? Hearing people take it for granted that they can simply call their friend, doctor, or whomever they wish. Deaf people cannot take that for granted. How they contact other people, deaf or hearing, and the issues that are involved were discussed in Chapters 2, 3, and 6. Thus, the problems researchers encounter can at least partially be turned to their advantage. The problems become a source of insight into the situation being studied.

I contacted and talked with more than 75 hearing-impaired people and 15 hearing individuals during the year that I gathered data. I interviewed young adults in their twenties and older deaf people in their sixties. I talked with husbands and wives, single people, divorced, and those who are single and living together. My contacts included college-educated people and grammar school graduates; those who depend on manual communication (signs and fingerspelling) and those who oppose it; adults who are deaf from birth and those who lost their hearing in their teens. I interviewed peddlers and professional people. Several people were interviewed more than once. One man, who could be called a key informant, was interviewed several times. Informal interviews were the primary way in which I gathered data about outsiders in a hearing world.

I hestiate to use the term "interview" in characterizing my interaction with the deaf respondents, because these encounters were often like a conversation. I used no specific questions and order of questions with everyone. Rather, general topics, which make up the bulk of this book, were examined. Background information about each respondent's childhood, school experiences, and work history were obtained. We gave and took in these sessions. Answers were explored in order to uncover how the deaf respondents felt and what they meant. I tried not to take for granted that certain phrases or signs meant the same to both of us. Sessions lasted from thirty minutes to four hours, with most being an hour to two. The interviews often ended with my talking about my experiences: having deaf parents or my wife's teaching deaf children. Thus, the deaf respondents and I exchanged information and experiences. I received far more from them than they received from me, though. Unfortunately, that is typically the case in social science research. The researcher takes, but gives very little back. The deaf people that I interviewed served both as respondents and informants. They responded to questions about their background, present activities, and feelings. Equally important, they informed me about activities of other deaf people and events within the deaf community. The specific incidents which my respondents related to me, especially these with hearing people, serve several purposes. They are used by the respondents in organizing their world, giving meaning to it, and then displaying that world and its meanings to others (e.g., researchers like myself). Those incidents should not be interpreted as occurring "everyday" or "all the time," though some may. More importantly, they occur often enough and are important enough to deaf people that they organize their world around those incidents and relate them to others. Those incidents are the concrete reference points for deaf people's feelings and perspectives.

I recorded these interviews with the deaf in two different ways. For those deaf people who did not have intelligible speech, I either took a *few* notes during our conversation or more often remembered what we talked about. When I arrived home or early the next morning, I typed my recollection of what was said and took place. Even had I wanted to, I could not have taken extensive notes during these interviews. When a deaf person signs it is difficult to take notes at the same time. One must watch their signing. This point would seem relatively obvious. However, an interpreter at a state university mentioned to me that a professor could not understand why a deaf student could not take her own notes, since she had this interpreter in class. One can look down to take notes and still hear the speaker. One cannot look down and still see the signer. To take notes between answers disrupts the flow of the conversation. Therefore I seldom took notes.

Some deaf people had intelligible speech. I tape-recorded many of these interviews and later transcribed them. By intelligible speech I do not necessarily mean "normal" speech. Some respondents would be understood by most anyone. In other cases, only those familiar with the speech of deaf people would have an easy time understanding my respondents. Thus, even though I had no funds to hire a typist to transcribe my tapes, it would not have done much good anyway. Often I had to play several times a particularly difficult passage before I understood what was said. Other times I never did. Fortunately, they were few and appeared at relatively unimportant places in the interviews.

Later, I realized that the transcriptions of my tapes provided me only with the relatively insignificant exact wording of the conversations and not additional information about activities and meanings. It also provided me with a lot of meaningless work. I decided not to use a tape recorder for the remainder of the deaf respondents whose speech could have been taped. By then my confidence and ability in memorizing the conversations had also increased.

Many of the conversations with the members of the deaf community had to be translated from sign language to English for my notes and for excerpts used in this book. Because I was not concerned with a linguistic analysis of the conversations with the deaf people, translations were not as difficult as they could have been. What was important was to understand what deaf people meant, not how they signed it. Understanding, though, sometimes took several requests for repetition, as I noted before. Equally important was to convey their thoughts and feelings into English clearly so that I could understand them several months later, and if used in this book, so that they would be understood by the reader as I understood them. Obviously, one needs to know both sign language and English. My translations and reconstructions, though, are not the only ones possible. Others would also be faithful to the style and content of the original conversation. A study of that translation process would be important. All I can say is that, based on my personal experiences, I was able to do it. Thus, materials from my interviews with deaf respondents which are presented in the preceding chapters are verbatim excerpts, reconstructions faithful to the style and content of the original conversation, or a summary of what was said.

I also interviewed fifteen hearing people: ministers, counselors, teachers, and friends of deaf individuals. These interviews provided information from a hearing perspective. Though these people are familiar with the deaf and did provide useful data, I did not in my analysis allow their ideas to distort the experiences of the deaf. I used these interviews to generate ideas, to check hunches, and to complement what I learned from the deaf.

Though interviews have been my primary source of data, I have supplemented them with other methods. I attended several Friday and Saturday night gatherings of a club for the deaf in the Chicago area. I observed a winter carnival sponsored by another deaf-run organization. And I visited and participated in several meetings and outings sponsored by a senior citizens' club for the deaf in Chicago. Much of my activity was as a nonparticipating observer who casually watched poker games, movies, discussions among deaf individuals, and the like. At other times, I was drawn into conversations or talked and joked with people I knew or who knew me. Thus, in this part of my research I played both what Raymond Gold (1958) calls the participant-as-observer role and the observer-as-participant role. I never intentionally kept my identity a secret or mislead others about my purpose for being there.

While there are no local magazines or newspapers published by and for the deaf in Chicago (except for a religious publication which I was denied access to), I read national deaf publications for stories, incidents, and ideas. I was particularly interested in materials relating to encounters between the deaf and the hearing. I examined the published writings of deaf individuals in order to collect additional information. Newspaper articles or books about the deaf proved to be helpful at times. Thus, published materials supplemented my interviews and observations.

I checked my results in several ways. A deaf man whom I interviewed several times, a key informant, as I mentioned earlier, read a rough draft of this book and commented on it. Since leaving the Chicago area, my experiences with and knowledge of deaf people in other parts of the country were compared with what I found in Chicago. I have talked over my ideas with some deaf and hearing people and received their comments. Published writings by members of other deaf communities seem to corroborate my findings and analyses. These checks also provided me with further information.

LIMITATIONS

All research and results have limitations. Several should be mentioned here. This book is about the Chicago area deaf community. It is a case study and should be treated as such. No matter how accurately it depicts the Chicago deaf community, one should not unthinkingly generalize the results of the preceding chapters to other deaf communities. While I used the term "deaf community" throughout the book, it was a short-hand way of saying the "Chicago area deaf community." There are many deaf communities.

Many researchers might make the cautionary statement that I made above and then proceed to generalize it to other situations that they did not study. They would like their results to have a wider applicability. Results which are confined to a particular locale seem less useful than those that can be generalized across time and space. Thus, although my findings should not be matter-of-factly generalized, certain discussions and analyses are likely to characterize the social world of the deaf outside of Chicago.

The analysis of encounters between the deaf and the hearing presented in Chapters 5 and 6, the discussion of the deviance of peddling among the deaf in Chapter 4, and the examination of the identity of members of the deaf community in Chapter 3 transcend the Chicago deaf community. Many of the informants did not always live in the Chicago area. Casual conversations with deaf people in other parts of the country complement the findings from Chicago. Printed materials by and about the deaf which were used in those chapters concern events in other parts of the country. The results in those chapters are likely to characterize in general outsiders in a hearing world.

The discussion of the Chicago deaf community presented in Chapter 2 is more likely to be tied to that locale than the discussions in the other chapters. Certain broad features, such as what constitutes membership within the community, will probably be found in most deaf communities. More specific relationships may not be. For example, the black and white deaf form separate communities in Chicago. One respondent explained, though, that in a town in the Pacific Northwest there was much greater association between the white and black deaf than in Chicago. Whether that is true or not, patterns of interaction among the deaf can change according to differing circumstances— circumstances which may reflect the wider hearing world as well. Or, as I noted in Chapter 2, Chicago has had a long history of oral day school programs. Therefore, many deaf people in the area were educated in these programs. Some became speakers. Some became signers. Some remained "pure" oralists. While there are antagonisms between the speakers and signers, they know each other and are part of the same deaf community. Less populated areas have typically been served by residential programs. In some of their programs, signing was part of the communication method (often for the older students or for those who could not learn orally). In other programs where signing was not officially part of the educational method, students often signed to one another on the playground or in the dorms. In either case, most students would be prone to be signers as adults. In such areas, the relationship between signers and speakers may be different than in Chicago. Therefore, the discussion in Chapter 2 is probably more restricted to the Chicago area than the discussions in the other chapters.

This book rests heavily on the personal experiences of the people whom I interviewed and observed. However, I believe that the insights which I have drawn from those experiences are not limited to understanding their lives exclusively. Those insights can help us understand not only other outsiders in a hearing world, but also the hearing world. This book also rests heavily on my personal experiences. Without those experiences I doubt that I would have written this book. But as it is, I hope that it helps us better understand outsiders in a hearing world.

References

Adam, Barry D. (1978) The Survival of Domination: Inferiorization and Everyday Life. New York: Elsevier.

Altman, Dennis (1971) Homosexual: Oppression and Liberation. New York: Outerbridge & Dienstfrey.

Altshuler, Kenneth Z. and George S. Baroff (1963) "Educational background and vocational adjustment." Pp. 116-130 in John D. Rainer, Kenneth Z. Altshuler, and Franz J. Kallmann (eds.) Family and Mental Health Problems in a Deaf Population. New York: New York State Psychiatric Institute.

Ames, R. (1950) "Protest and irony in Negro folksong." Science and Society 14: 193-213.

Anderson, Glenn B. and Frank G. Bowe (1972) "Racism within the deaf community." American Annals of the Deaf 117: 617-619.

Argyle, Michael and Janet Dean (1965) ' Eye-contact, distance and affiliation." Sociometry 28: 289-304.

Barker, Roger G., Beatrice A. Wright, Lee Meyerson, and Mollie R. Gonick (1953) Adjustment to Physical Handicap and Illness: A Survey of the Social Psychology of Physique and Disability. New York: Social Science Research Council.

Barry, John R. (1973) 'The Physically Disabled." Pp. 99-115 in Don Spiegel and Patricia Keith-Spiegel (eds.) Outsiders USA: Original Essays on 24 Outgroups. San Francisco: Rinehart Press

Bauman, Richard and Joel Sherzer (eds.) (1974) Explorations in the Ethnography of Speaking. London: Cambridge University Press.

Becker Howard S. (1963) Outsiders: Studies in the Sociology of Deviance. New York: Free Press.

––– (1967) "Whose Side are We On?" Social Problems 14: 239-247.

––– (1974) "Labelling theory reconsidered." Pp. 41-66 in Paul Rock and Mary McIntosh (eds.) Deviance and Social Control. London: Tavistock.

Bell, Alexander Graham (1883) 'Upon the formation of a deaf variety of the human race." Presented to the National Academy of Sciences.

Bender, Ruth E. (1970) The Conquest of Deafness. Cleveland: The Press of Case Western Reserve University.

Best, Harry (1943) Deafness and the Deaf in the United States. New York: MacMillan.

Birch, Jack W. (1974) Mainstreaming: Educable Mentally Retarded Children in Regular Classrooms. Minneapolis: University of Minnesota Leadership Training Institute/Special Education.

Blauner, Robert (1972) Racial Oppression in America. New York: Harper & Row.

Block, Samuel A. (1968) 'Problems of deaf professional persons." American Annals of the Deaf 113: 60-69.

Boese, Robert J. (1971) "Native sign language and the problem of meaning. Ph.D. dissertation, University of California–Santa Barbara. (unpublished)

Bogdan, Robert and Douglas Biklen (1977) "Handicapism." Social Policy 7: 14-19.

Bowe, Frank and Martin Sternberg (1973) I'm Deaf Too: 12 Deaf Americans. Silver Spring, Maryland: National Association of the Deaf.

Bowe, Frank G., Marcus T. Delk, and Jerome D. Schein (1973) "Barriers to the full employment of deaf people in federal government." Journal of Rehabilitation of the Deaf 6: 1-15.

Bragg, Bernard (1973) "Ameslish–our American Heritage." American Annals of the Deaf 118: 672-674.

Brehm, Jack W. (1966) A Theory of Psychological Reactance. New York: Academic Press.

Brill, Richard G. (1975) "Mainstreaming: format or quality?" American Annals of the Deaf 120: 377-381.

Butler, Richard R. (1979) Personal communication.

Carroll, Thomas J. (1961) Blindness: What It Is What It Does, and How to Live With It. Boston: Little, Brown.

Chicago Sun Times (1975) May 31: 5.

Chomsky, Noam (1965) Aspects of the Theory of Syntax. Cambridge: MIT Press.

Cooley, Charles Horton (1902) Human Nature and the Social Order. New York: Scribner.

Coser, Lewis A. (1956) The Functions of Social Conflict. New York: Free Press.

Cowen, Emory L., Philip H. Bobrove, Alan M. Rockway, and John Stevenson (1967) "Development and evaluation of an attitudes to deafness scale." Journal of Personality and Social Psychology 6: 183-191.

Cowen, Emory L., Rita P. Underberg, and Ronald T. Verrillo (1958) "The development and testing of an attitude to blindness scale." Journal of Social Psychology 48: 297-304.

Craig. William N. and James L. Collins (eds.) (1970) "New vistas for competitive employment of deaf persons." Journal of Rehabilitation of the Deaf, Monograph 2.

Crammatte, Alan B. (1968) Deaf Persons in Professional Employment. Springfield, Illinois: Charles C Thomas.

——— (1970) "Insurance problems of deaf people." Pp. 23-32 in Robert L. Meyer (ed.) The Deaf Man and the Law. Washington, DC: Council of Organizations Serving the Deaf.

Croneberg, Carl G. (1976) "Sign language dialects." Pp. 313-319 in William C. Stokoe, Jr., Dorothy C. Casterline, and Carl G. Croneberg (eds.) A Dictionary of American Sign Language on Linguistic Principles. Silver Spring, Maryland: Linstock Press.

Dank, Barry M. (1971) "Coming out in the gay world." Psychiatry 34: 180-197.

Davis, Fred (1961) "Deviance disavowal: the management of strained interaction by the visibly handicapped " Social Problems 9: 120-132.

Davis, Hallowell and S. Richard Silverman (eds.) (1960) Hearing and Deafness. New York: Holt, Rinehart & Winston.

Day, Beth (1972) Sexual Life Between Blacks and Whites: The Roots of Racism. New York: World Publishing.

The Deaf American (1973) 25: 29.

The Deaf Lutheran (1974) 66, 4.

Dentler, Robert A. and Kai T. Erikson (1959) "The functions of deviance in groups." Social Problems 7: 98-107.

Dexter, Lewis Anthony (1964) "On the politics and sociology of stupidity in our society." Pp. 37-49 in Howard S. Becker (ed.) The Other Side: Perspectives on Deviance. New York: Free Press.

Douglas, Jack D. (1970) "Deviance and respectability: the social construction of moral meanings." Pp. 3-30 in Jack D. Douglas (ed.) Deviance and Respectability: The Social Construction of Moral Meanings. New York: Basic Books.

——— (1976) Investigative Social Research. Beverly Hills, California: Sage.

Durkheim, Emile (1960) The Division of Labor in Society (George Simpson, trans.). New York: Free Press.

——— (1966) The Rules of Sociological Method (Sarah Solovay and John Mueller, trans.; George E. G. Catlin, ed.). New York: Free Press.

Emerson, Joan P. (1970) "Nothing unusual is happening." Pp. 208-22 in Tamotsu Shibutani (ed.) Human Nature and Collective Behavior. Englewood Cliffs, New Jersey: Prentice-Hall.

Emerton, R. Greg and Gail Rothman (1978) "Attitudes towards deafness: hearing students at a hearing and deaf college." American Annals of the Deaf 123: 588-593.

Erikson. Kai T. (1964) "Notes on the Sociology of Deviance." Pp. 9-21 in Howard S. Becker (ed.) The Other Side. New York: Free Press.

Fant, Louis J., Jr. (1974) "Letter to the editor." American Annals of the Deaf 119: 299-301.

Fay. Edward A. (1879) "Miscellaneous." American Annals of the Deaf 24: 194.

The Frat (1953) February, March.

Freidson, Eliot (1966) "Disability as social deviance." Pp. 71-99 in Marvin B. Sussman (ed.) Sociology and Rehabilitation. Washington, DC: American Sociological Association.

Furfey, Paul Hanly and Thomas J. Harte (1964) Interaction of Deaf and Hearing in Frederick County, Maryland. Washington DC. Catholic University of America press.

——— (1968) Interaction of Deaf and Hearing in Baltimore City, Maryland. Washington, DC: Catholic University of America Press.

Furth, Hans G. (1966) Thinking Without Language. New York: Free Press.

——— (1971) "Linguistic deficiency and thinking: research with deaf subjects 1964-69." Psychological Bulletin 76: 58-72.

––– (1973) Deafness and Learning: A Psychosocial Approach. Belmont, California: Wadsworth.

Gans, Herbert (1962) The Urban Villagers. New York: Free Press.

Gmelch, George and Sharon Bohn Gmelch (1978) "Begging in Dublin: the strategies of a marginal urban occupation." Urban Life 6: 439-454.

Goffman, Erving (1959) The Presentation of Self in Everyday Life. Garden City, New York: Doubleday.

––– (1963) Stigma: Notes on the Management of Spoiled Identity. Englewood Cliffs, New Jersey: Prentice-Hall.

––– (1974) Frame Analysis. Cambridge: Harvard University Press.

Gold, Raymond L. (1958) "Roles In Sociological Field Observations.": Social Forces 36: 217-223.

Goode, Erich (1978) Deviant Behavior: An Interactionist Approach. Englewood Cliffs, New Jersey: Prentice-Hall.

Gouldner, Alvin W. (1970) The Coming Crisis of Western Sociology. New York: Avon.

Gowman, Alan G. (1956) "Blindness and the role of companion." Social Problems 4: 68-75.

Grant, Joseph W. (1970) "Recent legislation affecting the deaf." Pp. 33-35 in Robert L. Meyer (ed.) The Deaf Man and the Law. Washington. DC: Council of Organizations Serving the Deaf.

Greenfield. Meg (1979) "A study in success." Newsweek (October 8): 108.

Gruss, Louis (1940) "The legal position of the deaf in present-day society." The Volta Review 42: 826-829, 874.

––– (1941) "The legal position of the deaf in present-day society." The Volta Review 43: 29-32 76.

Gusfield, Joseph (1976) "The literary rhetoric of science: comedy and pathos in drinking driver research." American Sociological Review 41: 16-34.

Hall, Edward Twitchell (1959) The Silent Language. Garden City, New York: Doubleday.

––– (1966) The Hidden Dimension. Garden City, New York: Doubleday.

Hanks, Jane R. and L. M. Hanks, Jr. (1948) "The physically handicapped in certain non-occidental societies." Journal of Social Issues 4: 11-20.

Heath, G. Louis (1972) Red, Brown, and Black Demands for Better Education. Philadelphia: Westminster Press.

Heiss, Jerold and Susan Owens (1972) "Self-evaluations of blacks and whites." American Journal of Sociology 78: 360-370.

Hillery, George A., Jr. (1955) "Definitions of community: areas of agreement." Rural Sociology 20: 111-123.

Hirschi, Travis (1973) "Procedural rules and the study of deviant behavior." Social Problems 21: 159-173.

Hughes, Everett Cherrington (1945) "Dilemmas and contradictions of status." American Journal of Sociology 50: 353-359.

––– (1964) "Good people and dirty work." Pp. 23-36 in Howaru S. Becker (ed.) The Other Side: Perspectives on Deviance. New York: Free Press.

Humphreys, Laud (1972) Out of the Closets: The Sociology of Homosexual Liberation. Englewood Cliffs, New Jersey: Prentice-Hall.

Hyman, Herbert H. (1942) "The psychology of status." Archives of Psychology 269.

Hymes, Dell (1974) Foundations in Sociolinguistics: An Ethnographic Approach. Philadelphia: University of Pennsylvania Press.

International Telephone Directory of the Deaf (1974-1975) Indianapolis: Teletypewriter of the Deaf.

Jacobs, Leo M. (1974) A Deaf Adult Speaks Out. Washington, DC: Gallaudet College Press.

Jones, Ray L. (ed.) (1969) "The deaf man and the world." In Proceedings: National Forum II, Council of Organizations Serving the Deaf.

––– (1979) Personal communication.

Jones, Reginald L. (ed.) (1976) Mainstreaming and the Minority Child. Minneapolis: University of Minnesota Leadership Training Institute/Special Education.

Jordan, I. K., Gerilee Gustason. and Roslyn Rosen (1979) "An update on communication trends at programs for the deaf." American Annals of the Deaf 124: 350-357.

Kiefer, Christie W. (1974) Changing Cultures, Changing Lives: An Ethnographic Study of Three Generations of Japanese Americans. San Francisco: Jossey-Bass.

Kirchner, Carl J. (1980) Personal communication.

Kleck, Robert, Hiroshi Ono, and Albert H. Hastorf (1966) "The effects of physical deviance upon face to-face interaction." Human Relations 19: 425-436.

Kramer, Ernest (1963) "Judgment of personal characteristics and emotions from nonverbal properties of speech." Psychological Bulletin 60: 408-420.

Ladieu, Gloria, Dan L. Adler, and Tamara Dembo (1948) "Studies in adjustment to visible injuries: social acceptance of the injured." Journal of Social Issues 4: 55-61.

Ladieu, Glorida, Eugenia Haufmann, and Tamara Dembo (1947) "Studies in adjustment to visible injuries: evaluation of help by the injured." Journal of Abnormal and Social Psychology 42: 169-192.

Lambert, W. E., R. C. Hodgson, R. C. Gardner, and S. Fillenbaum (1960) "Evaluational reactions to spoken languages." Journal of Abnormal and Social Psychology 60: 44-51.

Langer, Ellen J., Susan Fiske, Shelley E. Taylor, And Benzion Chanowitz. (1976) "Stigma, staring, and discomfort: a novel-stimulus hypothesis." Journal of Experimental Social Psychology 12: 451-463.

Laslett, Barbara and Carol A. B. Warren (1975) "Losing weight: the organizational promotion of behavior change." Social Problems 23: 69-80.

Lemert, Edwin M. (1951) Social Pathology. New York: McGraw-Hill.

Letkemann, Peter (1973) Crime as Work. Englewood Cliffs, New Jersey: Prentice-Hall.

Levine, Edna Simon (1960) The Psychology of Deafness: Techniques of Appraisal for Rehabilitation. New York: Columbia University Press.

Levine, Martin P. (1979) "Gay ghetto." Journal of Homosexuality 4: 363-377.

Levitin, Teresa E. (1975) "Deviants as active participants in the labeling process: the visibly handicapped." Social Problems 22: 548-557.

Lindesmith, Alfred R., Anselm L. Strauss, and Norman K. Denzin (1975) Social Psychology. Hinsdale, Illinois: Dryden Press.

Long, Bud (1978) Everything About Deaf Peddlers. Dallas: Gluxlit Press.

Margolis, Richard J. (1971) "The losers." Pp. 148-162 in James C. Stone and Donald P. Denevi (eds.) Teaching Multi-Cultural Populations: Five Heritages. New York: Van Nostrand Reinhold.

Markowicz, Harry and James Woodward (1978) "Language and the maintenance of ethnic boundaries in the deaf community." Communication and Cognition 11: 29-38.

Matza, David (1969) Becoming Deviant. Englewood Cliffs, New Jersey: Prentice-Hall.

McCall, George J. and J. L. Simmons (1966) Identities and Interactions. New York: Free Press.

McSweeney, Joan (1975) "Chicago's society on signs: report of an evening." The Deaf American 27: 11-12 19.

Mead, George H. (1934) Mind, Self, and Society. Chicago: University of Chicago Press.

Meadow, Kathryn (1972) "Sociolinguistics, sign language, and the deaf sub-culture." Pp. 19-33 in Terrence J. O'Rourke (ed.) Psycholinguistics and Total Communication: The State of the Art. (n.p.): American Annals of the Deaf.

Merrill, Edward C., Jr. (1979) "A deaf presence in education." Presented at the Eighth Congress of the World Federation of the Deaf, Varna, Bulgaria.

Meyerson, Lee (1948) "Physical disability as a social psychological problem." Journal of Social Issues 4: 2-10.

Mills, C. Wright (1959) The Sociological Imagination. New York: Oxford University Press.

Minar, David W. and Scott Greer (1969) The Concept of Community: Readings with Interpretation. Chicago: Aldine.

Mindel, Eugene D. and McCay Vernon (1971) The Deaf Child and His Family. Silver Springs, Maryland: National Association of the Deaf.

Moores, Donald F. (1972) "Communication—some unanswered questions and some unquestioned answers." Pp. 1-10 in Terrence J. O'Rourke (ed.) Psycholinguistics and Total Communication: The State of the Art. (n.p.): American Annals of the Deaf.

Moyer, Mary (1975) "Research on communication distance with deaf and hearing subjects." Pp. 37-8 in Eugene Bergman (ed.) The Role of Research and the Cultural and Social Orientation of the Deaf. Washington, DC: Gallaudet College Press.

Myers, Lowell J. (1964) The Law and the Deaf. Washington, DC: U.S. Department of Health, Education, and Welfare, Vocational Rehabilitation Administration.

Myklebust, Helmer R. (1964) The Psychology of Deafness: Sensory Deprivation, Learning, and Adjustment. New York: Grune & Stratton.

Nash, Jeffrey E. (1976) "Some sociolinguistic aspects of deaf educational policy." Sociological Focus 9: 349-360

Newsweek (1979) September 17: 73.

Oberman, C. Esco (1965) A History of Vocational Rehabilitation in America. Minneapolis: Denison.

Oral Deaf Adults Section Handbook (1975) Washington, DC: Alexander Graham Bell Association for the Deaf.

O'Rourke, Terrence J. (ed.) (1972) Psycholinguistics and Total Communication:

The State of the Art. (n.p.): American Annals of the Deaf.

Padden, Carol and Harry Markowicz (1975) "Crossing cultural group boundaries into the deaf community: Presented at the Conference on Culture and Communication, Temple University, Philadelphia.

Pettigrew, Thomas F. (1964) A Profile of the Negro American. Princeton, New Jersey: Litton.

Phillips, Derek L. (1971) Knowledge From What? Theories and Methods in Social Research. Skokie, Illinois: Rand McNally.

Pimentel, Albert T. (1979) Personal communication.

Pintner, Rudolph (1929) "Speech and Speech-Reading Tests for the Deaf." Journal of Applied Psychology 13: 220-225.

Plummer, Kenneth (1975) Sexual Stigma: An Interactionist Account. London: Routledge & Keagan Paul.

Ponse, Barbara (1977) "Secrecy in the lesbian world." Pp. 53-78 in Carol Warren (ed.) Sexuality: Encounters, Identities and Relationships. Beverly Hills, California: Sage.

Poplin, Dennis E. (1972) Communities: A Survey of Theories and Methods of Research. New York: Macmillan.

Psathas, George (1976) "On the mobility orientations and navigation of blind persons." Presented at Northwestern University, November 4.

Ransford H. Edward (1970) "Skin color, life chances, and anti-white attitudes." Social Problems 18: 164-179.

Reynolds, Maynard C. (ed.) (1977) Mainstreaming: Origins and Implications. Reston Virginia: Council for Exceptional Children.

Richardson, Stephen A. (1969) "The effect of physical disability on the socialization of a child." Pp. 1047-1064 in David A. Goslin (ed.) Handbook of Socialization Theory and Research. Skokie, Illinois: Rand McNally.

Richardson, Stephen A., Norman Goodman, Albert H. Hastorf, and Sanford M. Dornbusch (1961) "Cultural uniformity in reaction to physical disabilities." American Sociological Review 26: 241 247.

Riemer, Jeffrey W. (1977) "Varieties of opportunistic research." Urban Life 5: 467-477.

Safilios-Rothschild, Constantina (1970) The Sociology and Social Psychology of Disability and Rehabilitation. New York: Random House.

Sagarin, Edward (1969) Odd Man In: Societies of Deviants in America. Chicago: Quadrangle Books.

——— (1975) Deviants and Deviance: An Introduction to the Study of Disvalued People and Behavior. New York: Praeger.

Sattler, Jerome M. (1970) "Racial 'experimenter effects' in experimentation, testing, interviewing, and psychotherapy." Psychological Bulletin 73: 137-160.

Schegloff, Emanuel A. (1968) "Sequencing in conversational openings." American Anthropologist 70: 1075-1095.

Schein, Jerome D. (1968) The Deaf Community: Studies in the Social Psychology of Deafness. Washington, DC: Gallaudet College Press.

Schein, Jerome D. and Marcus T. Delk, Jr. (1974) The Deaf Population of the United States. Silver Springs, Maryland: National Association of the Deaf.

Schiff, William and Stephen Thayer (1974) "A eye for an ear? social perception, nonverbal communication, and deafness." Rehabilitation Psychology 21: 50-70.

Schiffrin, Deborah (1977) "Opening encounters." American Sociological Review 42: 679-691.

Schlesinger, Hilde S. and Kathryn P. Meadow (1972) Sound and Sign: Childhood Deafness and Mental Health. Berkeley: University of California Press.

Schowe, B. M. (1979) Identity Crisis in Deafness: A Humanistic Perspective. Tempe, Arizona: Scholars Press.

Scott, Robert A. (1969a) The Making of Blind Men: A Study of Adult Socialization. New York: Russell Sage.

· —— (1969b) "The socialization of blind children." Pp. 1025-1045 in David A. Goslin (ed.) Handbook of Socialization Theory and Research. Skokie, Illinois: Rand McNally.

——— (1976) "Deviance, sanctions, and social integration in small-scale societies." Social Forces 54: 604-620.

Simmel, Georg (1955) Conflict (Kurt H. Wolff, trans.). New York: Free Press.

Simmons, J. L. (1965) "Public stereotypes of deviants." Social Problems 13: 223-232.

Simmons, Roberta G. (1978) "Blacks and high self-esteem: a puzzle." Social Psychology 41: 54-57.

Simpson, George Eaton and J. Milton Yinger (1972) Racial and Cultural Minorities: An Analysis of Prejudice and Discrimination. New York: Harper & Row.

Special Learning Corporation (1978) Readings in Mainstreaming. Guilford, Connecticut.

Stevenson, Elwood A., Ignatius Bjorlee, T. C. Forrester, Clarence D. O'Connor, and Irving S. Fusfeld (1938) "Report of the conference committee on nomenclature." American Annals of the Deaf 83: 1-3.

Stokoe, William C. and Robbin M. Battison (1975) Sign Language, Mental Health, and Satisfying Interaction. Chicago: David T. Siegel Institute for Communicative Disorders, Michael Reese Hospital and Medical Center.

Stokoe, William C., Dorothy C. Casterline, and Carl G. Croneberg (1976) A Dictionary of American Sign Language on Linguistic Principles. Silver Spring, Maryland: Linstock Press.

Strauss, Anselm and Barney G. Glaser (1975) Chronic Illness and the Quality of Life. St. Louis: Mosby.

Sullivan, Frank (1976) Personal communication.

Sussman, Allen E. (1973) An Investigation into the Relationship Between Self Concepts of Deaf Adults and Their Perceived Attitudes Toward Deafness. Ph.D. dissertation, New York University. (unpublished)

——— and Douglas J. N. Burke (1968) "Problems of deaf professional persons with the deaf community." American Annals of the Deaf 113: 77-87.

Tallman, Irving (1976) Passion, Action and Politics: A Perspective on Social Problems and Social Problem Solving. San Francisco: Freeman.

Thompson, Daniel C. (1974) Sociology of the Black Experience. Westport, Connecticut: Greenwood Press.

Tidyman, Ernest (1974) Dummy. Boston: Little, Brown.

Trybus, Raymond J. and Michael A. Karchmer (1977) "School achievement scores of hearing impaired children: national data on achievement status and growth patterns." American Annals of the Deaf 122: 62-69.

Turner, Ralph (1972) "Deviance avowal as neutralization of commitment." Social Problems 19: 308-321.

Udry, J. Richard, Karl E. Bauman, and Charles Chase (1971) "Skin color, status, and mate selection." American Journal of Sociology 76: 722-733.

U.S. Bureau of the Census (1973) "Characteristics of the population." Part 15, Illinois-Section 1 in Census of Population, Volume 1. Washington, DC: Government Printing Office.

––– (1976) "Estimates of the population of Illinois counties and metropolitan areas: July 1, 1974 and 1975." Current Population Reports series P-26, number 75-13. Washington, DC: Government Printing Office.

Valentine, Charles A. (1968) Culture and Poverty: Critique and Counter-Proposal. Chicago: University of Chicago Press.

Vernon, McCay (1967) "Relationship of language to the thinking process." Archives of General Psychiatry 16: 325-333.

––– (1969) "The final report." Pp. 13-37 in Roy R. Grinker (ed.) Psychiatric Diagnosis, Therapy and Research on the Psychotic Deaf. Washington, DC: U.S. Department of Health, Education, and Welfare.

Vernon, McCay and Charles C. Estes (1975) "Deaf leadership and political activism." The Deaf American 28: 3-6.

Voysey, Margaret (1972) "Impression management by parents with disabled children." Journal of Health and Social Behavior 13: 80-89.

Warfield, Frances (1948) Cotton in My Ears. New York: Viking.

Warren, Carol A. B. (1972) "Observing the gay community." Pp. 139-163 in Jack D. Douglas (ed.) Research on Deviance. New York: Random House.

––– (1974) Identity and Community in the Gay World. New York: John Wiley.

Webb, Eugene J., Donald T. Campbell Richard D. Schwartz, and Lee Sechrest (1966) Unobtrusive Measures: Nonreactive Research in the Social Sciences. Skokie, Illinois: Rand McNally

Weinberg, Martin S. (1965) "Sexual modesty, social meanings, and the nudist camp." Social Problems 12: 311-318.

––– (1968) 'The problems of midgets and dwarfs and organizational remedies: a study of little people of America." Journal of Health and Social Behavior 9: 65-71.

––– (1970) "The male homosexual: age-related variations in social and psychological characteristics." Social Problems 17: 527-537.

White, Ralph K., Beatrice A. Wright and Tamara Dembo (1948) "Studies in adjustment to visible injuries: evaluation of curiosity by the injured." Journal of Abnormal and Social Psychology 43: 13-28.

Williams, J. Allen, Jr. (1964) "Interviewing respondent interaction: a study of bias in the information interview." Sociometry 27: 338-352.

Woodward, James C., Jr. (1973) "Deaf awareness." Sign Language Studies 3: 57-59.

––– (1976) "Black southern signing." Language in Society 5: 211-218.

––– (1978) "Historical bases of American sign language." Pp. 333-348 in P. Siple (ed.) Understanding Language Through Sign Language. New York: Academic Press.

––– (1979) Signs of Sexual Behavior: An Introduction to Some Sex-Related

Vocabulary in American Sign Language. Silver Spring, Maryland: T. J. Publishers.

Wright Beatrice A. (1960) Physical Disability—A Psychological Approach. New York: Harper & Row.

Wright David (1969) Deafness: A Personal Account. London: Allen Lane.

Yarrow, Marian Radke (1958) "Personality development and minority group membership." Pp. 451-474 in Marshall Sklare (ed.) The Jews: Social Patterns of an American Group. New York: Free Press.

About the Author

PAUL C. HIGGINS is Assistant Professor of Sociology at the University of South Carolina. He has published articles on delinquency, deviance, and disability, as well as coedited *Health, Illness, and Medicine: A Reader in Medical Sociology* with Gary L. Albrecht.